Conceptual PHYSICS

Next-Time Questions
Paul G. Hewitt and Helen Yan

Prentice Hall

Needham, Massachusetts
Upper Saddle River, New Jersey
Glenview, Illinois

ISBN 0-13-0542

2 3 4 5 6 7 8 9 10   05 04 03 0

Contents

USE THESE MASTERS TO MAKE COPIES FOR POSTING, OR TO MAKE TRANSPARENCIES FOR OVERHEAD PROJECTION. END YOUR CLASS WITH A QUESTION --- THEN BEGIN THE NEXT WITH AN ANSWER.

THERE IS A TOTAL OF 98 QUESTIONS IN ALL --- AT LEAST ONE FOR EACH CHAPTER.

ENJOY!

1. HUMAN BEINGS WILL NEVER SET FOOT ON THE MOON.

2. SOME OF THE LAWS THAT GOVERN NATURE CANNOT BE DETECTED BY SCIENTISTS.

3. IT IS QUITE POSSIBLE THAT IN SOME OTHER GALAXY THE LAWS OF PHYSICS ARE FUNDAMENTALLY DIFFERENT THAN THE LAWS WE ARE ACQUAINTED WITH IN THIS GALAXY.

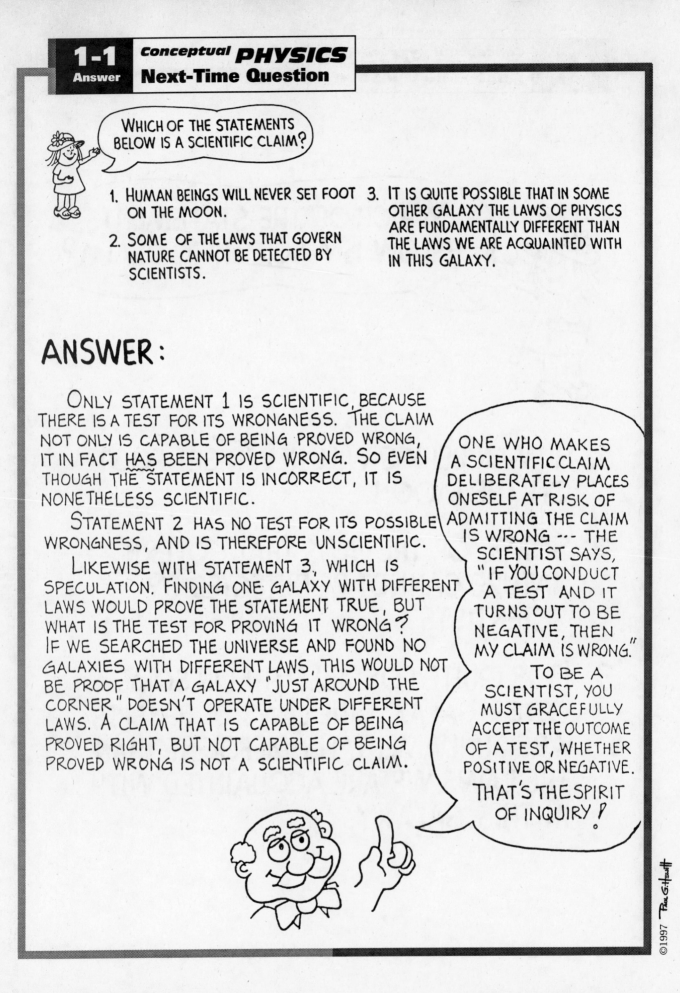

WHICH OF THE STATEMENTS BELOW IS A SCIENTIFIC CLAIM?

1. HUMAN BEINGS WILL NEVER SET FOOT ON THE MOON.

2. SOME OF THE LAWS THAT GOVERN NATURE CANNOT BE DETECTED BY SCIENTISTS.

3. IT IS QUITE POSSIBLE THAT IN SOME OTHER GALAXY THE LAWS OF PHYSICS ARE FUNDAMENTALLY DIFFERENT THAN THE LAWS WE ARE ACQUAINTED WITH IN THIS GALAXY.

ANSWER:

ONLY STATEMENT 1 IS SCIENTIFIC, BECAUSE THERE IS A TEST FOR ITS WRONGNESS. THE CLAIM NOT ONLY IS CAPABLE OF BEING PROVED WRONG, IT IN FACT HAS BEEN PROVED WRONG. SO EVEN THOUGH THE STATEMENT IS INCORRECT, IT IS NONETHELESS SCIENTIFIC.

STATEMENT 2 HAS NO TEST FOR ITS POSSIBLE WRONGNESS, AND IS THEREFORE UNSCIENTIFIC.

LIKEWISE WITH STATEMENT 3, WHICH IS SPECULATION. FINDING ONE GALAXY WITH DIFFERENT LAWS WOULD PROVE THE STATEMENT TRUE, BUT WHAT IS THE TEST FOR PROVING IT WRONG? IF WE SEARCHED THE UNIVERSE AND FOUND NO GALAXIES WITH DIFFERENT LAWS, THIS WOULD NOT BE PROOF THAT A GALAXY "JUST AROUND THE CORNER" DOESN'T OPERATE UNDER DIFFERENT LAWS. A CLAIM THAT IS CAPABLE OF BEING PROVED RIGHT, BUT NOT CAPABLE OF BEING PROVED WRONG IS NOT A SCIENTIFIC CLAIM.

ONE WHO MAKES A SCIENTIFIC CLAIM DELIBERATELY PLACES ONESELF AT RISK OF ADMITTING THE CLAIM IS WRONG --- THE SCIENTIST SAYS, "IF YOU CONDUCT A TEST AND IT TURNS OUT TO BE NEGATIVE, THEN MY CLAIM IS WRONG." TO BE A SCIENTIST, YOU MUST GRACEFULLY ACCEPT THE OUTCOME OF A TEST, WHETHER POSITIVE OR NEGATIVE. THAT'S THE SPIRIT OF INQUIRY!

©1997

WHEN THE 10 km/h BIKES ARE 20 km APART, A BEE BEGINS FLYING FROM ONE WHEEL TO THE OTHER AT A STEADY SPEED OF 30 km/h. WHEN IT GETS TO THE WHEEL, IT ABRUPTLY TURNS AROUND AND FLIES BACK TO TOUCH THE FIRST WHEEL, THEN TURNS AROUND AND KEEPS REPEATING THE BACK-AND-FORTH TRIP UNTIL THE BIKES MEET, AND ⸮SQUISH!⸮

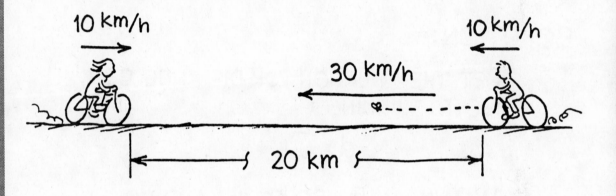

QUESTION

HOW MANY KILOMETERS DID THE BEE TRAVEL IN ITS TOTAL BACK-AND-FORTH TRIPS?

WHEN THE 10 km/h BIKES ARE 20 km APART, A BEE BEGINS FLYING FROM ONE WHEEL TO THE OTHER AT A STEADY SPEED OF 30 km/h. WHEN IT GETS TO THE WHEEL, IT ABRUPTLY TURNS AROUND AND FLIES BACK TO TOUCH THE FIRST WHEEL, THEN TURNS AROUND AND KEEPS REPEATING THE BACK-AND-FORTH TRIP UNTIL THE BIKES MEET, AND ⸾SQUISH!⸾

QUESTION

HOW MANY KILOMETERS DID THE BEE TRAVEL IN ITS TOTAL BACK-AND-FORTH TRIPS?

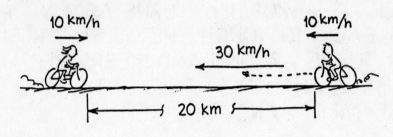

SOLUTION:

LET THE EQUATION FOR DISTANCE BE A GUIDE TO THINKING:

$$d = \bar{v}\, t$$

WE KNOW $\bar{v} = 30$ km/h, AND WE MUST FIND THE TIME t. WE CONSIDER THE SAME TIME FOR THE BIKES AND SEE IT TAKES 1 HOUR FOR THEM TO MEET, SINCE EACH TRAVELS 10 km AT A SPEED OF 10 km/h. SO,

$$d = \bar{v}\, t = 30 \text{ km/h} \times 1 \text{ h} = 30 \text{ km}$$

THE BEE TRAVELED A TOTAL OF 30 km.

Addison-Wesley Publishing Company, Inc.

An airplane makes a straight back-and-forth round trip, always at the same airspeed, between two cities. If it encounters a mild steady tailwind going, and the same steady headwind returning, will the round trip take more, less, or the same time as with no wind?

©1997 Paul G. Hewitt

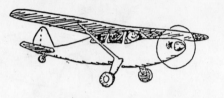

An airplane makes a straight back-and-forth round trip, always at the same airspeed, between two cities. If it encounters a mild steady tailwind going, and the same steady headwind returning, will the round trip take more, less, or the same time as with no wind?

Answer:

The windy trip will take more time, as any numerical example will show. Suppose the cities are 600 km apart, and the airspeed of the plane is 300 km/h (relative to still air). Then time each way with no wind is 2 hours. Roundtrip time is 4 hours. Consider a 100 km/h tailwind going, so groundspeed is (300 + 100) km/h. Then the

time is $\dfrac{600 \text{ km}}{400 \text{ km/h}}$, or 1 hour and 30 minutes.

Returning, groundspeed is (300 − 100) km/h, and the

time is $\dfrac{600 \text{ km}}{200 \text{ km/h}}$, or 3 hours.

The windy round trip takes 4.5 hours—longer than with no wind at all.

Since this is one of those "greater than, equal to, or less than" questions, use exaggerated values—like wind speed equalling airspeed. Then it's easy to see the plane cannot make the return trip with such a headwind. As windspeed approaches airspeed, roundtrip time approaches infinity. For any windspeed, roundtrip time is always greater than with no wind.

©1997

A ZOOKEEPER DEVISES A RUBBER-BAND GUN TO SHOOT FOOD TO A MONKEY WHO IS TOO SHY TO COME DOWN FROM THE TREES.

IF THE MONKEY DOES NOT MOVE, SHOULD THE KEEPER AIM ABOVE, AT, OR BELOW THE MONKEY?

IF THE MONKEY LETS GO OF THE BRANCH AT THE INSTANT THE KEEPER SHOOTS THE FOOD, SHOULD THE KEEPER AIM ABOVE, AT, OR BELOW THE MONKEY TO GET FOOD TO THE MONKEY IN MID-AIR?

BANANA

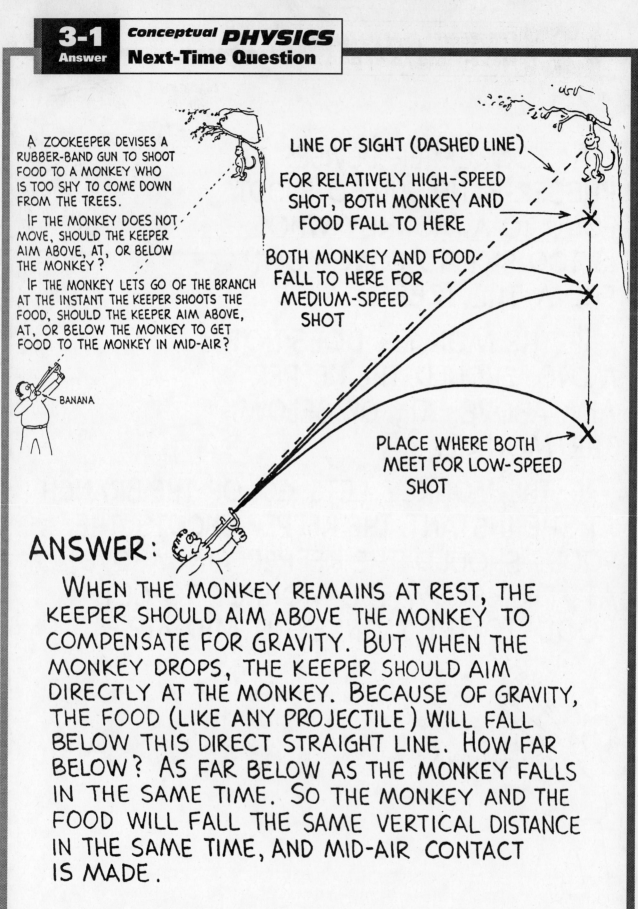

A ZOOKEEPER DEVISES A RUBBER-BAND GUN TO SHOOT FOOD TO A MONKEY WHO IS TOO SHY TO COME DOWN FROM THE TREES.

IF THE MONKEY DOES NOT MOVE, SHOULD THE KEEPER AIM ABOVE, AT, OR BELOW THE MONKEY?

IF THE MONKEY LETS GO OF THE BRANCH AT THE INSTANT THE KEEPER SHOOTS THE FOOD, SHOULD THE KEEPER AIM ABOVE, AT, OR BELOW THE MONKEY TO GET FOOD TO THE MONKEY IN MID-AIR?

BANANA

LINE OF SIGHT (DASHED LINE)

FOR RELATIVELY HIGH-SPEED SHOT, BOTH MONKEY AND FOOD FALL TO HERE

BOTH MONKEY AND FOOD FALL TO HERE FOR MEDIUM-SPEED SHOT

PLACE WHERE BOTH MEET FOR LOW-SPEED SHOT

ANSWER:

WHEN THE MONKEY REMAINS AT REST, THE KEEPER SHOULD AIM ABOVE THE MONKEY TO COMPENSATE FOR GRAVITY. BUT WHEN THE MONKEY DROPS, THE KEEPER SHOULD AIM DIRECTLY AT THE MONKEY. BECAUSE OF GRAVITY, THE FOOD (LIKE ANY PROJECTILE) WILL FALL BELOW THIS DIRECT STRAIGHT LINE. HOW FAR BELOW? AS FAR BELOW AS THE MONKEY FALLS IN THE SAME TIME. SO THE MONKEY AND THE FOOD WILL FALL THE SAME VERTICAL DISTANCE IN THE SAME TIME, AND MID-AIR CONTACT IS MADE.

Addison-Wesley Publishing Company, Inc.

The speed of an airplane relative to the ground is affected by wind. When an airplane flies in the direction of a wind (tailwind), it has a greater groundspeed. When an airplane flies directly into a wind (headwind), it has a smaller groundspeed.

Suppose an airplane flies with a 90-degree crosswind (the nose pointing in a direction perpendicular to the wind direction). Will its groundspeed be more, less, or the same as in still air?

The speed of an airplane relative to the ground is affected by wind. When an airplane flies in the direction of a wind (tailwind), it has a greater groundspeed. When an airplane flies directly into a wind (headwind), it has a smaller groundspeed.

Suppose an airplane flies with a 90-degree crosswind (the nose pointing in a direction perpendicular to the wind direction). Will its groundspeed be more, less, or the same as in still air?

Groundspeed will be greater. When directions as well as magnitudes of speeds are considered, we're into vectors. The resulting speed can be found by finding the resultant velocity via vector rules. The diagram shows a sample vector that represents the magnitude and direction of the airspeed, and another that represents the velocity of windspeed. The resultant is the diagonal of the parallelogram so formed. In this case, the parallelogram is a rectangle. The Pythagorean Theorem ($c^2 = a^2 + b^2$) gives the magnitude of the resultant. The angle can be found with a protractor, or a bit of trigonometry.

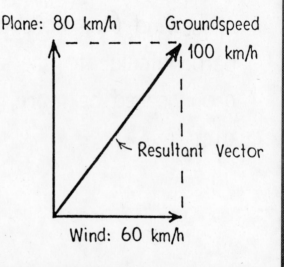

Plane: 80 km/h   Groundspeed
                  100 km/h
← Resultant Vector
Wind: 60 km/h

Addison-Wesley Publishing Company, Inc.

©1997

THE BOY ON THE TOWER THROWS A BALL 20 METERS DOWNRANGE AS SHOWN.

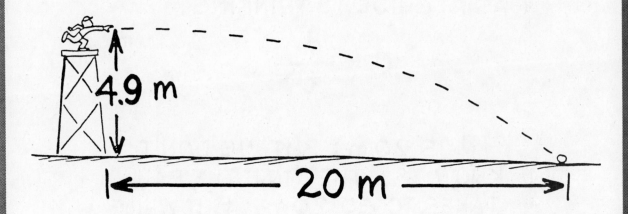

4.9 m

20 m

WHAT IS HIS PITCHING SPEED?

©1997

THE BOY ON THE TOWER THROWS
A BALL 20 METERS DOWNRANGE
AS SHOWN.

WHAT IS HIS PITCHING SPEED?

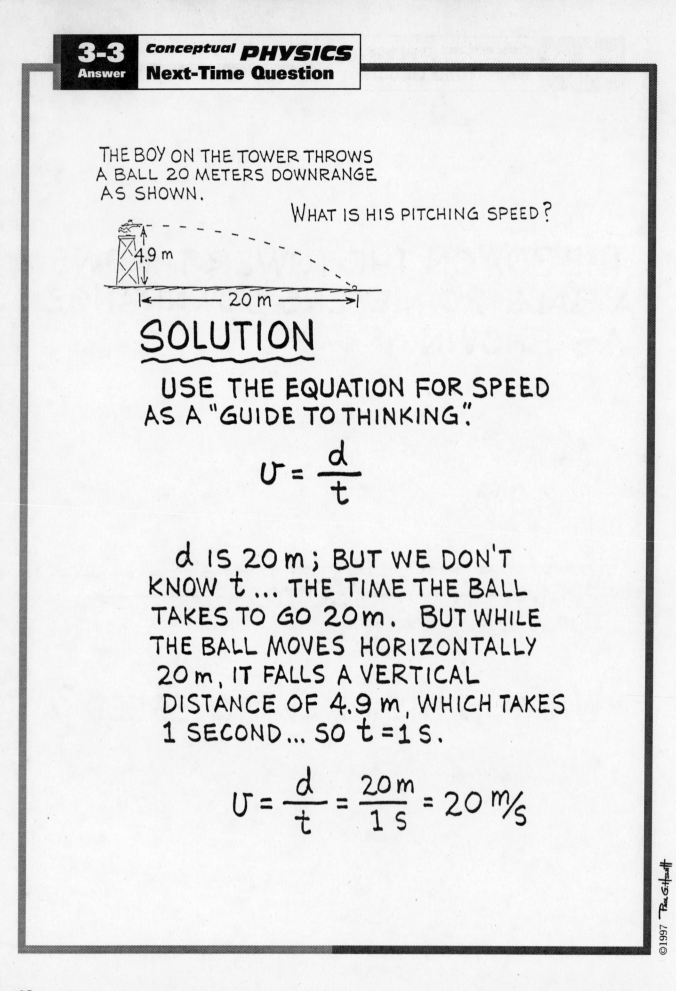

4.9 m

20 m

SOLUTION

USE THE EQUATION FOR SPEED
AS A "GUIDE TO THINKING".

$$v = \frac{d}{t}$$

d IS 20 m; BUT WE DON'T
KNOW t ... THE TIME THE BALL
TAKES TO GO 20m. BUT WHILE
THE BALL MOVES HORIZONTALLY
20 m, IT FALLS A VERTICAL
DISTANCE OF 4.9 m, WHICH TAKES
1 SECOND ... SO t = 1 s.

$$v = \frac{d}{t} = \frac{20m}{1s} = 20\ m/s$$

Addison-Wesley Publishing Company, Inc.

WHEN THE PELLET FIRED INTO THE SPIRAL TUBE EMERGES, WHICH PATH WILL IT FOLLOW? (NEGLECT GRAVITY)

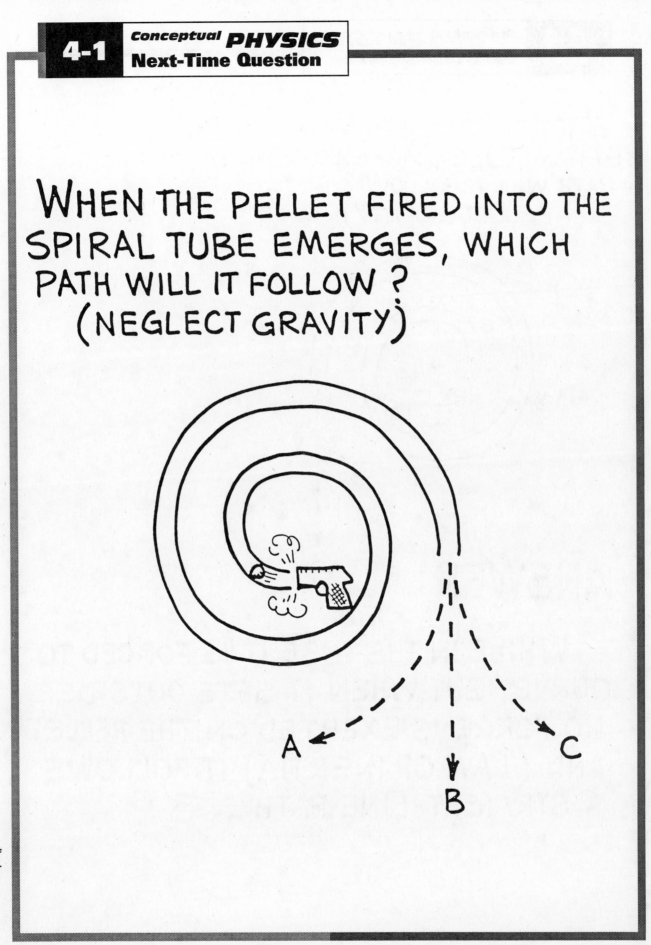

WHEN THE PELLET FIRED INTO THE
SPIRAL TUBE EMERGES, WHICH
PATH WILL IT FOLLOW ?
   (NEGLECT GRAVITY)

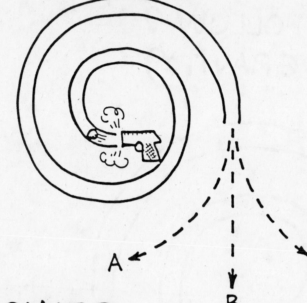

ANSWER:

WHILE IN THE TUBE IT IS FORCED TO
CURVE, BUT WHEN IT GETS OUTSIDE,
NO FORCE IS EXERTED ON THE PELLET
AND (LAW OF INERTIA) IT FOLLOWS
A STRAIGHT-LINE PATH... B !

Addison-Wesley Publishing Company, Inc.

WHEN THE BALL AT THE END OF THE STRING SWINGS TO ITS LOWEST POINT, THE STRING IS CUT BY A SHARP RAZOR.

WHICH PATH WILL THE BALL THEN FOLLOW?

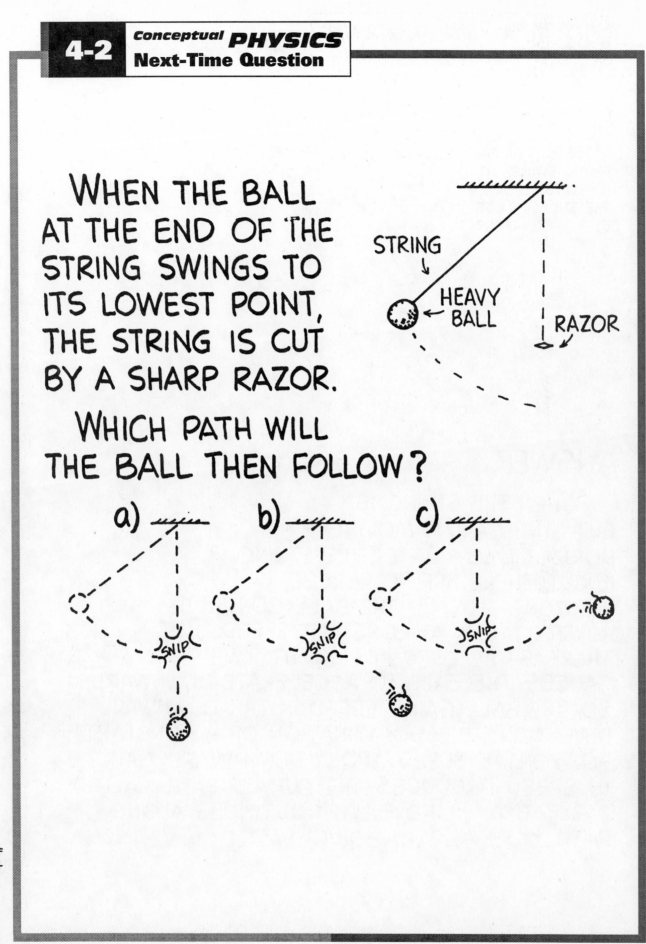

STRING

HEAVY BALL

RAZOR

a) SNIP

b) SNIP

c) SNIP

©1997

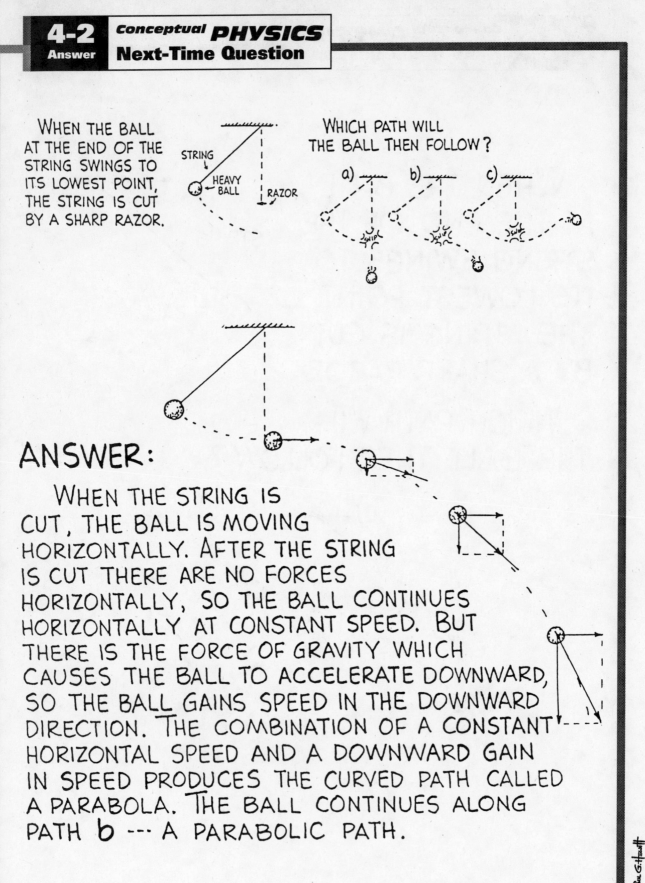

WHEN THE BALL AT THE END OF THE STRING SWINGS TO ITS LOWEST POINT, THE STRING IS CUT BY A SHARP RAZOR.

STRING
HEAVY BALL
RAZOR

WHICH PATH WILL THE BALL THEN FOLLOW?

a)   b)   c)

ANSWER:

WHEN THE STRING IS CUT, THE BALL IS MOVING HORIZONTALLY. AFTER THE STRING IS CUT THERE ARE NO FORCES HORIZONTALLY, SO THE BALL CONTINUES HORIZONTALLY AT CONSTANT SPEED. BUT THERE IS THE FORCE OF GRAVITY WHICH CAUSES THE BALL TO ACCELERATE DOWNWARD, SO THE BALL GAINS SPEED IN THE DOWNWARD DIRECTION. THE COMBINATION OF A CONSTANT HORIZONTAL SPEED AND A DOWNWARD GAIN IN SPEED PRODUCES THE CURVED PATH CALLED A PARABOLA. THE BALL CONTINUES ALONG PATH **b** --- A PARABOLIC PATH.

Addison-Wesley Publishing Company, Inc.

She holds the book stationary against the wall as shown. Friction on the book by the wall acts

(a) upward.
(b) downward.
(c) can't say.

She holds the book stationary against the wall as shown. Friction on the book by the wall acts

(a) upward.
(b) downward.
(c) can't say.

The answer is (c); can't say. If she barely pushes on the book so it tends to slide downward, then friction acts upward (because the vertical component of her push is less than the weight of the book). If she pushes with just enough force so the book tends not to slide at all (when the vertical component of push equals weight), then no wall friction acts. Or if she pushes hard enough so the book tends to slide upward (when the vertical component of push is greater than the book's weight), then friction acts downward. The question is ambiguous.

Addison-Wesley Publishing Company, Inc.

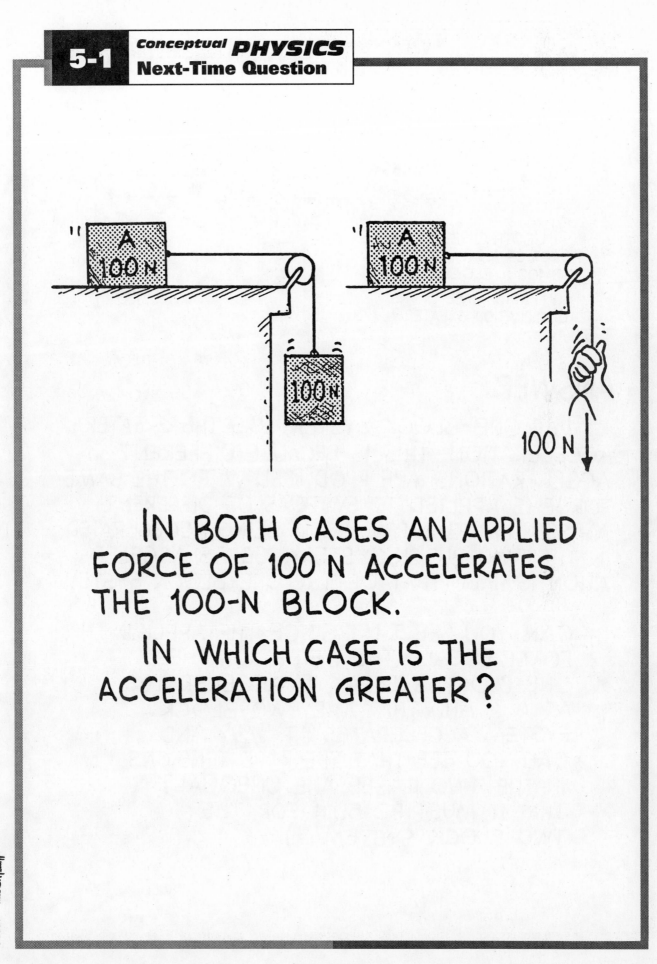

IN BOTH CASES AN APPLIED FORCE OF 100 N ACCELERATES THE 100-N BLOCK.

IN WHICH CASE IS THE ACCELERATION GREATER?

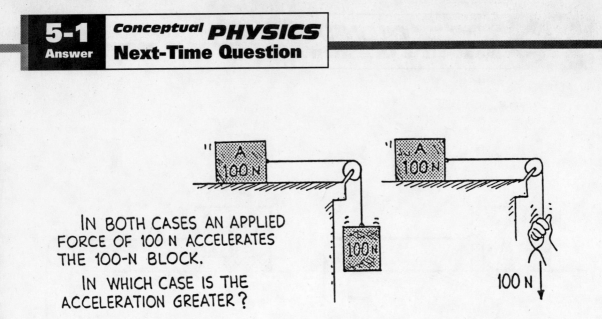

In BOTH CASES AN APPLIED
FORCE OF 100 N ACCELERATES
THE 100-N BLOCK.

IN WHICH CASE IS THE
ACCELERATION GREATER?

100 N

ANSWER:

THE ONE-BLOCK SYSTEM HAS THE GREATER
ACCELERATION. THIS IS BECAUSE DIFFERENT
ACCELERATIONS ARE PRODUCED WHEN THE SAME
FORCE IS APPLIED TO SYSTEMS OF DIFFERENT
MASS. TWICE THE MASS IS BEING ACCELERATED
IN THE TWO-BLOCK SYSTEM, SO ITS ACCELER-
ATION IS HALF THAT OF THE ONE-BLOCK SYSTEM.

(CAN YOU SEE THAT SINCE THE APPLIED
FORCE EQUALS THE WEIGHT OF THE
ONE-BLOCK SYSTEM, IT ACCELERATES
AT g? AND THAT THE TWO-BLOCK
SYSTEM ACCELERATES AT $g/2$? AND
CAN YOU SEE THAT THE ROPE TENSIONS
IN THE TWO CASES ARE UNEQUAL?
THAT IT MUST BE 50 N FOR THE
TWO-BLOCK SYSTEM?)

©1997

The brakes are slammed on a speeding truck and it skids to a stop. If the truck were heavily loaded so it had twice the total mass, the skidding distance would be

a) the same

b) 1 ½ times as far

c) twice as far

d) four times as far

The brakes are slammed on a speeding truck and it skids to a stop. If the truck were heavily loaded so it had twice the total mass, the skidding distance would be

a) the same

b) 1½ times as far

c) twice as far

d) four times as far

MOMENTUM TRANSFER

Answer:

Twice the mass means the skidding tires will bear against the road with twice the force, which results in twice the friction. Twice as much friction acting on twice as much mass produces the same deceleration and hence the same stopping distance.

Twice the *speed* would produce four times the stopping distance.

WHICH ENCOUNTERS
THE GREATER FORCE
OF AIR RESISTANCE---
A FALLING ELEPHANT
OR A FALLING FEATHER?

©1997

WHICH ENCOUNTERS
THE GREATER FORCE
OF AIR RESISTANCE---
A FALLING ELEPHANT
OR A FALLING FEATHER?

ANSWER:

THERE IS A GREATER FORCE OF AIR RESISTANCE ON THE FALLING ELEPHANT, WHICH "PLOWS THROUGH" MORE AIR THAN THE FEATHER IN GETTING TO THE GROUND. THE ELEPHANT ENCOUNTERS SEVERAL NEWTONS OF AIR RESISTANCE, WHICH COMPARED TO ITS HUGE WEIGHT HAS PRACTICALLY NO EFFECT ON ITS RATE OF FALL. ONLY A SMALL FRACTION OF A NEWTON ACTS ON THE FEATHER, BUT THE EFFECT IS SIGNIFICANT BECAUSE THE FEATHER WEIGHS ONLY A FRACTION OF A NEWTON.

REMEMBER TO DISTINGUISH BETWEEN A FORCE ITSELF AND THE EFFECT IT PRODUCES!

Addison-Wesley Publishing Company, Inc.

WHAT WILL BE THE ACCELERATION OF A ROCK THROWN STRAIGHT UPWARD AT THE MOMENT IT REACHES THE TIPPITY-TOP OF ITS TRAJECTORY?

©1997

WHAT WILL BE THE
ACCELERATION OF
A ROCK THROWN
STRAIGHT UPWARD
AT THE MOMENT
IT REACHES THE
TIPPITY-TOP OF
ITS TRAJECTORY?

ANSWER:

ALTHOUGH ITS SPEED AND
VELOCITY AT THE TOP WILL BOTH
INSTANTANEOUSLY BE ZERO, ITS
ACCELERATION WILL BE g, OR 9.8 m/s². REMEMBER,
ACCELERATION IS NOT SPEED OR VELOCITY --- IT IS
THE *RATE* AT WHICH VELOCITY CHANGES. A
MOMENT BEFORE OR AFTER THE ROCK REACHES
THE TOP, IT IS MOVING, WHICH IS EVIDENCE THAT
ITS VELOCITY IS CHANGING AT EVERY INSTANT.
THE ROCK UNDERGOES A CHANGE AS IT PASSES
THROUGH THE ZERO VALUE OF VELOCITY JUST AS
IT UNDERGOES THE SAME RATE OF CHANGE
PASSING THROUGH ANY OTHER VALUE OF VELOCITY.

OR LOOK AT IT VIA NEWTON'S 2ND LAW.
AT THE TOP OR ANYWHERE IN ITS PATH, THE
ROCK HAS BOTH WEIGHT AND MASS, AND

$$a = \frac{F}{m} = \frac{mg}{m} = g \ .$$

©1997

As she falls faster and faster through the <u>air</u>, her acceleration
a) increases
b) decreases
c) remains the same

©1997 Paul G. Hewitt

As she falls faster and faster
through the <u>air</u>, her acceleration
  a) increases
  b) decreases
  c) remains the same

The answer is b:

Acceleration decreases because the net force on her
decreases. Net force is equal to her weight minus her
air resistance, and since air resistance increases with
increasing speed, net force and hence acceleration
decrease. By Newton's 2nd law:

$$a = \frac{F_{NET}}{m} = \frac{(mg - R)}{m}$$

where **mg** is her weight, and **R** is the air resistance
she encounters. As **R** increases, **a** decreases.
Note that if she falls fast enough so that **R = mg**,
a = 0, then with no acceleration she falls at constant
velocity.

Go an extra step in the equation for Newton's 2nd
law (divide **mg** and **R** by **m**) and get

$$a = g - \frac{R}{m}$$

Note that the acceleration **a** will always be less
than **g** if air resistance **R** impedes falling. Only when
R = 0 does **a = g**.

© 1997

Addison-Wesley Publishing Company, Inc.

Two smooth balls of exactly the same size, one made of wood and the other of iron, are dropped from a high building to the ground below. The ball to encounter the greater force of air resistance on the way down is the

a) wooden ball

b) iron ball

c) ... both the same

©1997

Two smooth balls of exactly the same size, one made of wood and the other of iron, are dropped from a high building to the ground below. The ball to encounter the greater force of air resistance on the way down is the

a) wooden ball

b) iron ball

c) ... both the same

The answer is b:

Air resistance depends on both the size and speed of a falling object. Both balls have the same size, but the heavier iron ball falls faster through the air and encounters more air resistance in its fall.

Be careful to distinguish between the *amount* of air drag and the *effect* of that air drag. If the greater air drag on the faster ball is small compared to the weight of the ball, it won't be very effective in reducing acceleration. Like 2 newtons of air drag on a 20-newton ball has less effect on fall than 1 newton of air drag on a 2-newton ball.

1 N
2 N
2 N
20 N

Addison-Wesley Publishing Company, Inc.

A 1-kg ROCK IS THROWN AT 10 m/s STRAIGHT UPWARD. NEGLECTING AIR RESISTANCE, WHAT IS THE NET FORCE THAT ACTS ON IT WHEN IT IS HALF WAY TO THE TOP OF ITS PATH?

© 1997

A 1-kg ROCK IS THROWN AT 10 m/s STRAIGHT UPWARD. NEGLECTING AIR RESISTANCE, WHAT IS THE NET FORCE THAT ACTS ON IT WHEN IT IS HALF WAY TO THE TOP OF ITS PATH?

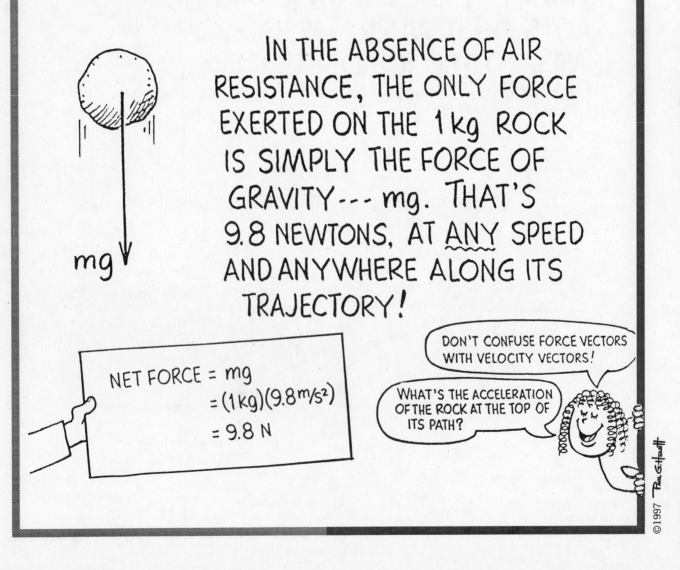

ANSWER:

IN THE ABSENCE OF AIR RESISTANCE, THE ONLY FORCE EXERTED ON THE 1 kg ROCK IS SIMPLY THE FORCE OF GRAVITY--- mg. THAT'S 9.8 NEWTONS, AT ANY SPEED AND ANYWHERE ALONG ITS TRAJECTORY!

NET FORCE = mg
= (1kg)(9.8 m/s²)
= 9.8 N

DON'T CONFUSE FORCE VECTORS WITH VELOCITY VECTORS!

WHAT'S THE ACCELERATION OF THE ROCK AT THE TOP OF ITS PATH?

©1997

FOR EVERY FORCE THERE EXISTS AN
EQUAL AND OPPOSITE FORCE. CONSIDER
ACTION AND REACTION FORCES IN THE
CASE OF A ROCK FALLING UNDER THE
INFLUENCE OF GRAVITY. IF ACTION
IS CONSIDERED TO BE THAT OF THE
EARTH PULLING DOWN ON THE ROCK,
CAN YOU CLEARLY IDENTIFY THE
REACTION FORCE ?

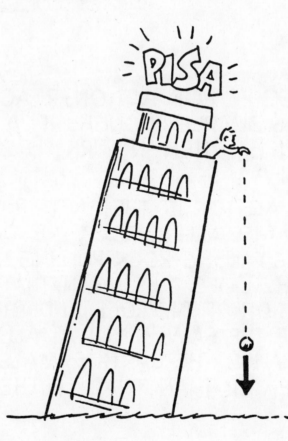

FOR EVERY FORCE THERE EXISTS AN EQUAL AND OPPOSITE FORCE. CONSIDER ACTION AND REACTION FORCES IN THE CASE OF A ROCK FALLING UNDER THE INFLUENCE OF GRAVITY. IF ACTION IS CONSIDERED TO BE THAT OF THE EARTH PULLING DOWN ON THE ROCK, CAN YOU CLEARLY IDENTIFY THE REACTION FORCE?

ANSWER:

THE RECIPE FOR ACTION-REACTION FORCES IS SIMPLE ENOUGH: IF **A** EXERTS FORCE ON **B**, THEN IN TURN, **B** EXERTS FORCE ON **A**.

SO IF ACTION IS THE EARTH PULLING DOWN ON THE FALLING ROCK, REACTION IS SIMPLY THE FALLING ROCK PULLING UP ON THE EARTH. DOES THIS MEAN THAT THE ACCELERATION OF THE ROCK AND THE EARTH SHOULD BE THE SAME? NOT AT ALL, BUT ONLY BECAUSE THE EARTH'S MASS IS SO MUCH GREATER THAN THAT OF THE FALLING ROCK.

©1997

Addison-Wesley Publishing Company, Inc.

IF A MACK TRUCK AND A
VOLKSWAGEN HAVE A HEAD-ON
COLLISION, WHICH VEHICLE
WILL EXPERIENCE THE GREATER
IMPACT FORCE?

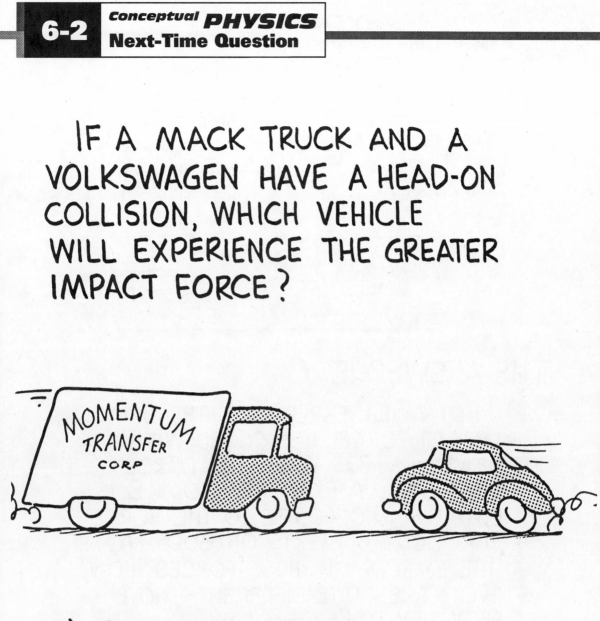

a) THE MACK TRUCK

b) THE VOLKSWAGEN

c) BOTH THE SAME

d) ... IT DEPENDS ON OTHER FACTORS

IF A MACK TRUCK AND A
VOLKSWAGEN HAVE A HEAD-ON
COLLISION, WHICH VEHICLE
WILL EXPERIENCE THE GREATER
IMPACT FORCE?

a) THE MACK TRUCK
b) THE VOLKSWAGEN
c) BOTH THE SAME
d) ...IT DEPENDS ON OTHER FACTORS

THE ANSWER IS C :

BOTH WILL EXPERIENCE THE SAME
IMPACT FORCE, IN ACCORD WITH
NEWTON'S 3RD LAW. THE FORCE
THAT BODY **A** EXERTS ON BODY **B** IS
EQUAL AND OPPOSITE TO THE FORCE
THAT BODY **B** EXERTS ON BODY **A**.
THE *EFFECTS* OF THESE FORCES, HOW-
EVER, ARE QUITE DIFFERENT --- NOTE
FROM NEWTON'S 2ND LAW

$$\frac{F_{TRUCK}}{M_{TRUCK}} = a \;\; ; \;\; \frac{F_{CAR}}{m_{CAR}} = a$$

SO THE CAR DECELERATES MUCH
MORE THAN THE MASSIVE TRUCK.

©1997

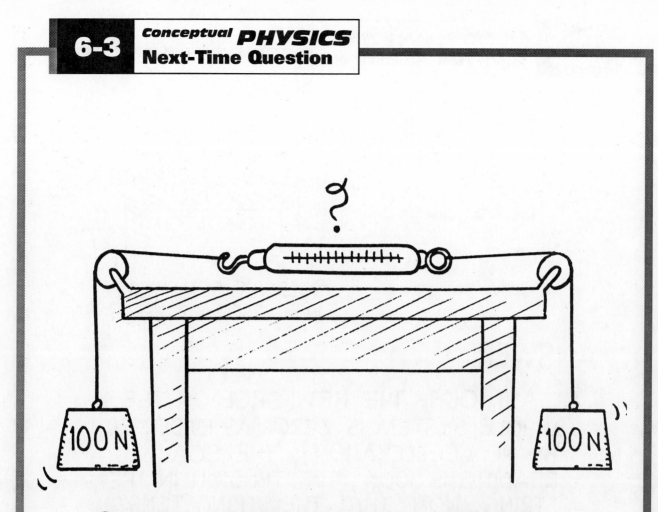

DOES THE SCALE READ
100n, 200n, OR ZERO?

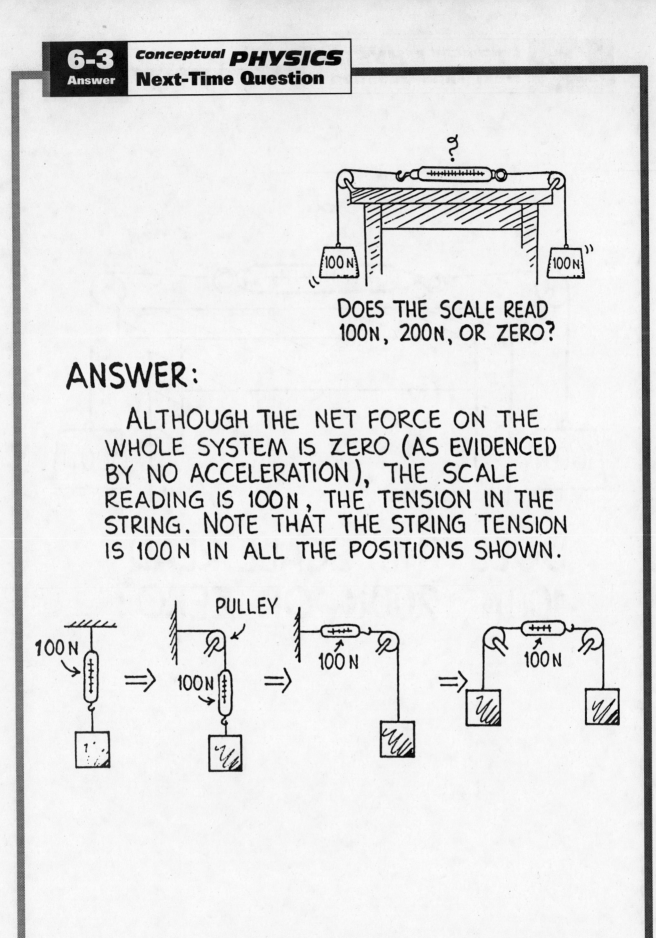

DOES THE SCALE READ
100N, 200N, OR ZERO?

ANSWER:

ALTHOUGH THE NET FORCE ON THE
WHOLE SYSTEM IS ZERO (AS EVIDENCED
BY NO ACCELERATION), THE SCALE
READING IS 100N, THE TENSION IN THE
STRING. NOTE THAT THE STRING TENSION
IS 100N IN ALL THE POSITIONS SHOWN.

©1997

Arnold Strongman and Suzie Small pull on opposite ends of a rope in a tug of war. The greatest force exerted on the rope is by

a) Arnold

b) Suzie

c) ... both the same

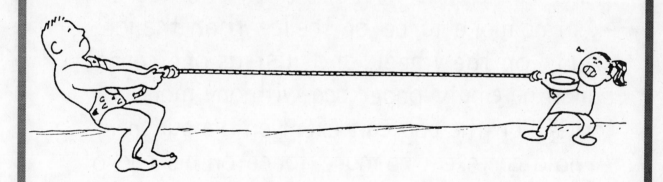

(Assume the rope's mass is negligible.)

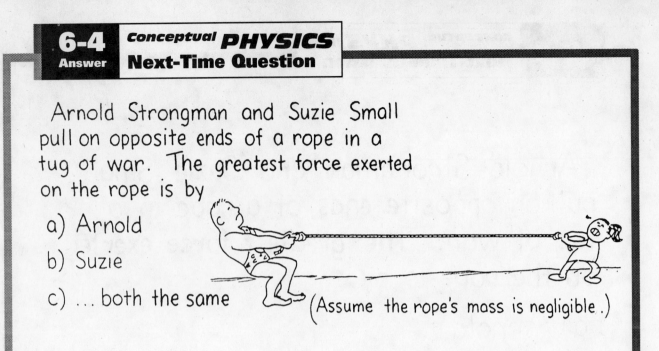

Arnold Strongman and Suzie Small pull on opposite ends of a rope in a tug of war. The greatest force exerted on the rope is by

a) Arnold

b) Suzie

c) ...both the same

(Assume the rope's mass is negligible.)

The answer is C:

Arnold can pull no harder on the rope than Suzie. Rope tension is the same all along the rope, including the ends. Just as a wheel on ice can exert no more force on the ice than the ice exerts on the wheel, and just as one cannot punch an empty paper bag with any more force than the bag can exert on the puncher, Arnold can exert no more force on his end of the rope than Suzie exerts on her end.

Arnold can push harder on the ground than Suzie can, so even though the pulls on the rope are the same, Arnold will likely win the tug of war!

©1997

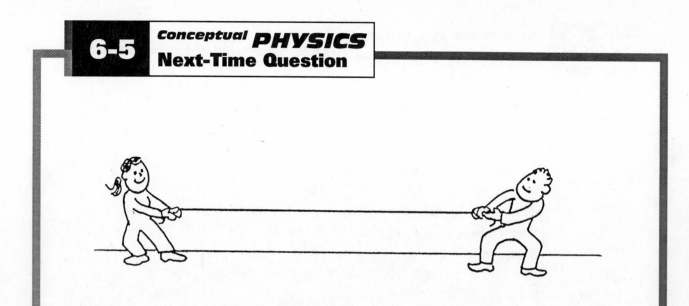

Two people of equal mass, 6 meters apart, attempt a tug of war on frictionless ice. If they pull on opposite ends of the rope with equal forces, each slides 3 meters to a point midway between them. Suppose instead that only one person pulls and the other fastens the rope around his or her waist. How far does each person slide?

(Neglect any effects of the rope's mass.)

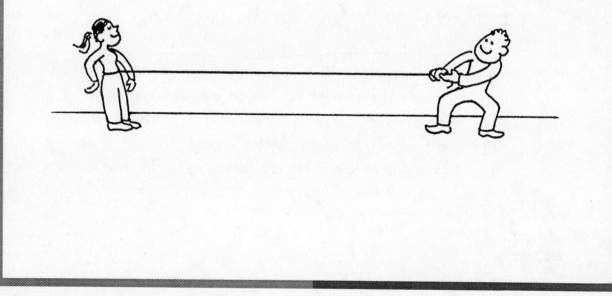

Two people of equal mass, 6 meters apart, attempt
a tug of war on frictionless ice. If they pull on
opposite ends of the rope with equal forces, each
slides 3 meters to a point midway between them.
Suppose instead that only one person pulls and the
other fastens the rope around his or her waist.
How far does each person slide?
(Neglect any effects of the rope's mass.)

Answer:

Each slides 3 meters, whether or not the pull is intentional.
At each end of the rope is an interaction governed by Newton's
third law. If the first person pulls on the rope with a certain
force, the rope pulls back on that person with the same force,
causing that person to accelerate. The force exerted by this
person on the rope is transmitted by the rope to become the
force exerted on the second person. So the second person is
acted on by the same magnitude of force as the first person,
and they accelerate equally (in opposite directions).

Another way to see this is to think of the center of mass
of the whole system of the two persons and the rope. This
center of mass is midway between the two persons. Since
no net force acts on this system from outside, its center
of mass will remain fixed, and that is where the two
persons will meet.

Addison-Wesley Publishing Company, Inc.

©1997

Conceptual PHYSICS
Next-Time Question

Consider the apple at rest on the table. If we call the gravitational force exerted on the apple *action*, what is the *reaction force* according to Newton's 3rd Law?

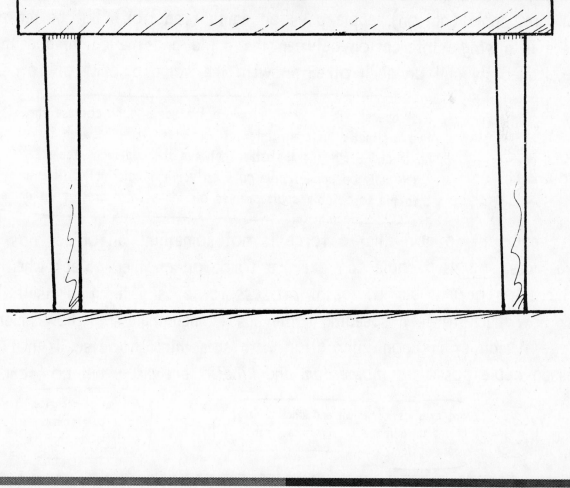

©1997 Paul G. Hewitt

Consider the apple at rest on the table. If we call the gravitational force exerted on the apple *action*, what is the *reaction force* according to Newton's 3rd Law?

Answer:

The reaction force is the apple gravitationally pulling on the earth (and NOT the support force by the table!). To identify a pair of action-reaction forces in any situation, first identify the pair of interacting objects involved. Something is interacting with something else. In this case the whole earth is interacting (gravitationally) with the apple. So the earth pulls downward on the apple (call it action), while the apple pulls upward on the earth (reaction). Simply put, earth pulls on apple (action); apple pulls on earth (reaction). But better put, there is a *single* interaction between the apple and the earth, and they simultaneously pull on each other -- with the *same* amount of force.

Just because their magnitudes are the same, don't confuse the two distinctly different interactions -- the one between the apple and earth and the other between the apple and table. *Earth pulls on apple; apple pulls on earth*, is distinctly different than the force pair *apple presses on table; table presses on apple.*

It's important to note that a force is not something an object *has*, like mass. A tossed apple can *exert* a force on another object when interaction occurs, but it doesn't *possess* force as a thing in itself. To ask how much force a speeding apple has is meaningless -- how much force it can exert upon interaction with something, however, is not. A tossed apple possesses *momentum* and *kinetic energy* -- but not force.

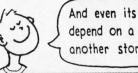

And even its momentum and kinetic energy depend on a *frame of reference*...but that's another story!

An action-reaction force pair comprises a <u>single</u> interaction.

©1997

JOCKO, WHO HAS A MASS OF 60 kg AND STANDS AT REST ON ICE, CATCHES A 20 kg BALL THAT IS THROWN TO HIM AT 10 km/h. HOW FAST DOES JOCKO AND THE BALL MOVE ACROSS THE ICE?

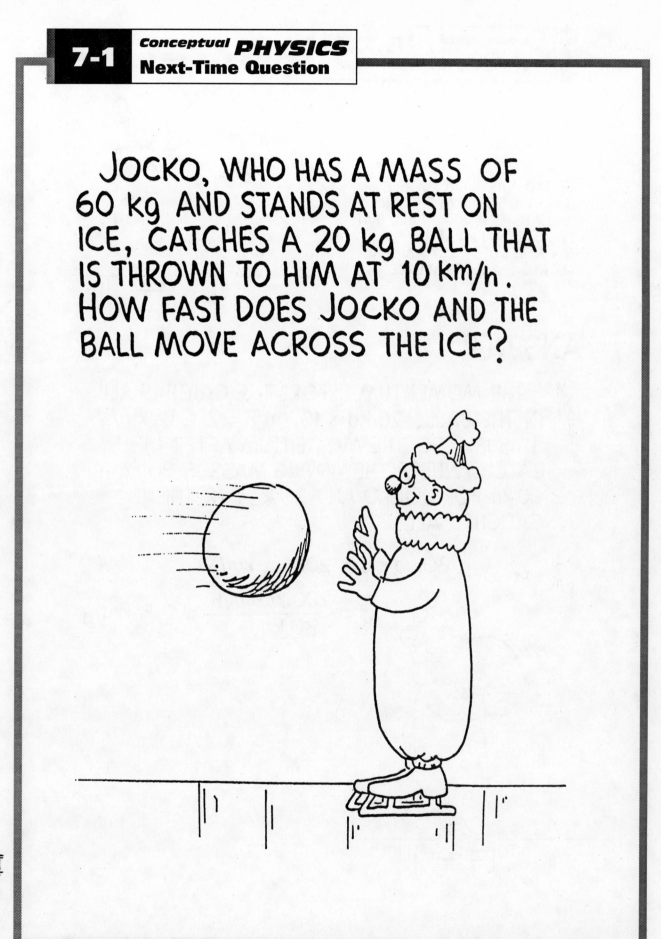

JOCKO, WHO HAS A MASS OF 60 kg AND STANDS AT REST ON ICE, CATCHES A 20 kg BALL THAT IS THROWN TO HIM AT 10 km/h. HOW FAST DOES JOCKO AND THE BALL MOVE ACROSS THE ICE?

ANSWER:

THE MOMENTUM BEFORE THE CATCH IS ALL IN THE BALL, 20 kg × 10 km/h = 200 kg·km/h. THIS IS ALSO THE MOMENTUM AFTER THE CATCH, WHERE THE MOVING MASS IS 80 kg··· 60 kg FOR JOCKO AND 20 kg FOR THE CAUGHT BALL.

$$80 \text{ kg} \times \upsilon = 200 \text{ kg·km/h}$$

$$\upsilon = \frac{200 \text{ kg·km/h}}{80 \text{ kg}} = 2.5 \text{ km/h}$$

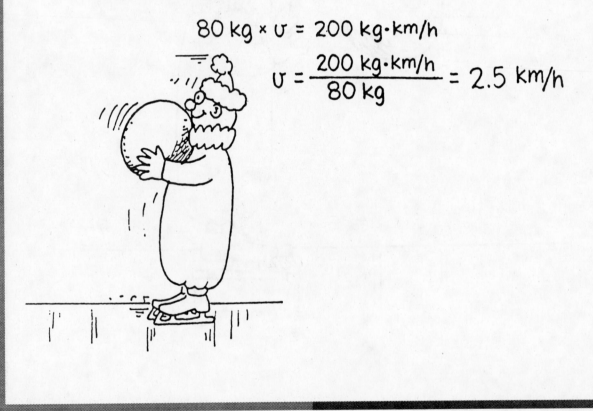

FOR THE SAME FORCE, WHY IS THE SPEED OF A CANNONBALL GREATER WHEN SHOT FROM A CANNON WITH A LONGER BARREL?

©1997

FOR THE SAME FORCE, WHY IS THE SPEED OF A CANNONBALL GREATER WHEN SHOT FROM A CANNON WITH A LONGER BARREL?

ANSWER:

THERE ARE TWO MAIN REASONS FOR THE GREATER SPEED. A CANNONBALL WITH GREATER SPEED HAS GREATER MOMENTUM AND GREATER KINETIC ENERGY. HOW DOES IT GET GREATER MOMENTUM FOR THE SAME APPLIED FORCE? BY A GREATER IMPULSE, WHICH IS "FORCE × TIME." THE TIME DURING WHICH THE FORCE ACTS IS LONGER IN THE LONG BARREL! OR HOW DOES THE CANNON-BALL GET MORE KINETIC ENERGY? BY GREATER WORK, WHICH IS "FORCE × DISTANCE." THE GREATER DISTANCE THE FORCE ACTS IN THE BARREL PRODUCES MORE WORK = MORE KINETIC ENERGY!

©1997

Addison-Wesley Publishing Company, Inc.

IF A SMALL OBJECT IS PLACED ON A ROTATING DISK (LIKE A RECORD PLAYER) IT WILL SLIDE OFF THE EDGE. SUPPOSE YOU FASTEN A BAR ON THE DISK AS SHOWN IN THE TOP VIEW, AND ALLOW THE OBJECT TO SLIDE FROM AN INSIDE POSITION, ALONG THE BAR, AND OFF THE EDGE. WHICH OF THE PATHS SHOWN WOULD BE MOST LIKELY?

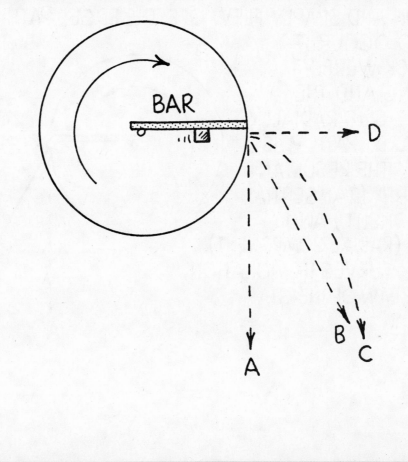

©1997

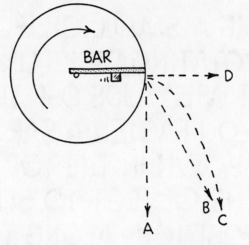

IF A SMALL OBJECT IS PLACED ON A ROTATING DISK (LIKE A RECORD PLAYER) IT WILL SLIDE OFF THE EDGE. SUPPOSE YOU FASTEN A BAR ON THE DISK AS SHOWN IN THE TOP VIEW, AND ALLOW THE OBJECT TO SLIDE FROM AN INSIDE POSITION, ALONG THE BAR, AND OFF THE EDGE. WHICH OF THE PATHS SHOWN WOULD BE MOST LIKELY?

ANSWER:

PATH **B** IS THE LIKELY PATH. PATH **A** WOULD BE THE CASE IF THE OBJECT HAD NO RADIAL COMPONENT OF MOTION AND SIMPLY FLEW OFF THE EDGE. PATH **D** WOULD OCCUR IF THE DISK WEREN'T SPINNING AND THE OBJECT SLID RADIALLY OUTWARD. PATH **B** IS SIMPLY THE RESULTANT OF PATH **A** (TANGENTIAL COMPONENT) AND PATH **D** (RADIAL COMPONENT). PATH **C** CURVES IN VIOLATION OF THE LAW OF INERTIA.

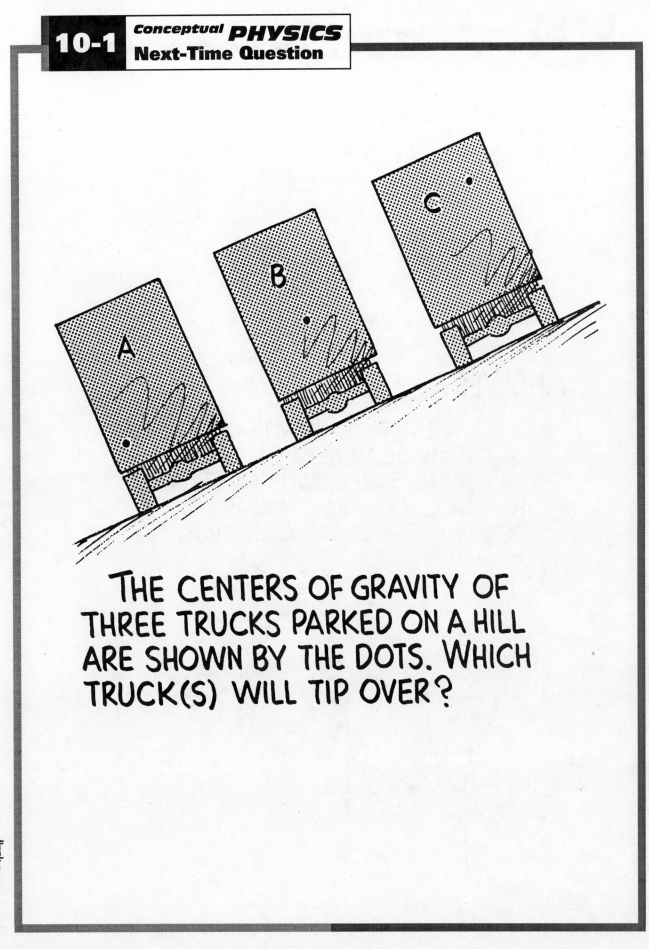

THE CENTERS OF GRAVITY OF
THREE TRUCKS PARKED ON A HILL
ARE SHOWN BY THE DOTS. WHICH
TRUCK(S) WILL TIP OVER?

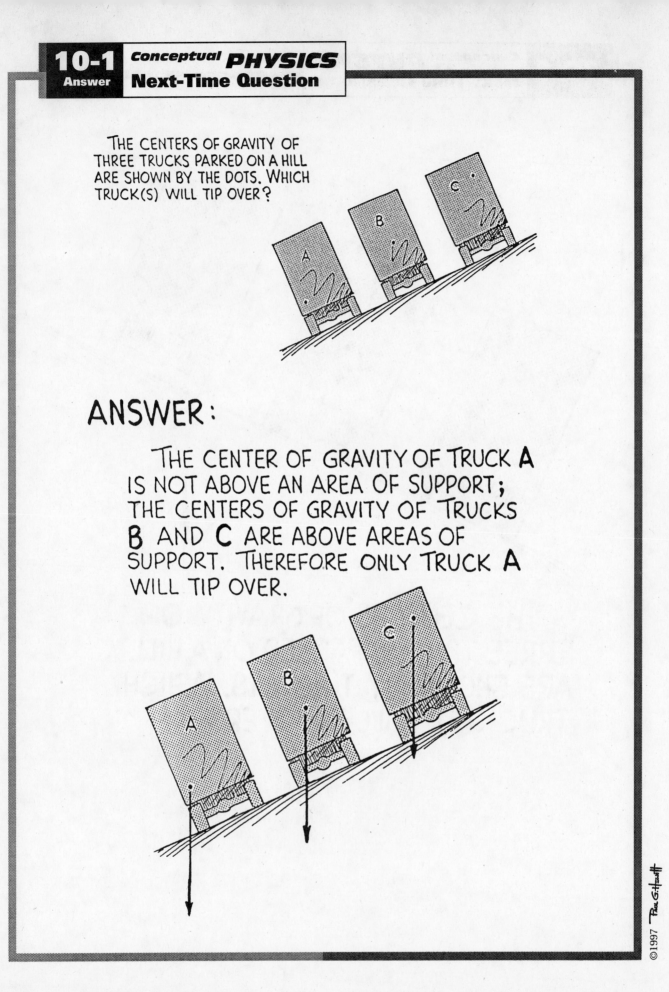

THE CENTERS OF GRAVITY OF
THREE TRUCKS PARKED ON A HILL
ARE SHOWN BY THE DOTS. WHICH
TRUCK(S) WILL TIP OVER?

ANSWER:

THE CENTER OF GRAVITY OF TRUCK **A**
IS NOT ABOVE AN AREA OF SUPPORT;
THE CENTERS OF GRAVITY OF TRUCKS
B AND **C** ARE ABOVE AREAS OF
SUPPORT. THEREFORE ONLY TRUCK **A**
WILL TIP OVER.

Addison-Wesley Publishing Company, Inc.
©1997

When she shakes the basket full of berries, the larger berries will

a) sink to the bottom

b) go to the top

c) not particularly sink nor rise, but like the smaller berries, be randomly distributed

©1997

When she shakes the basket full of berries, the larger berries will

a) sink to the bottom

b) go to the top

c) not particularly sink nor rise, but like the smaller berries, be randomly distributed

The answer is b :

As the berries are shaken, gaps open up between and beneath them -- some large and some small gaps -- but mostly small gaps. Since only small berries can move down into the small gaps, over time the large berries are nudged to the top.

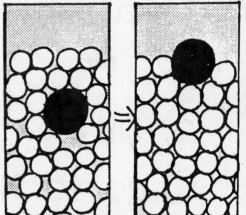

Interestingly enough, even denser objects move to the top in this way. Gentle motions in the ground nudge heavy rocks to the surface -- a source of frustration to gardeners.

©1997

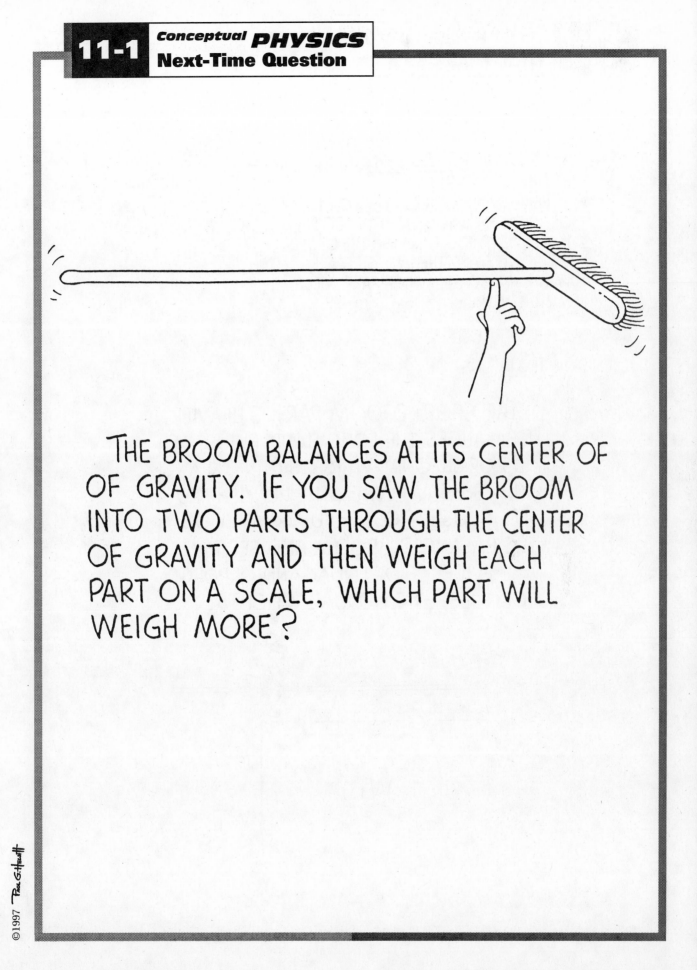

THE BROOM BALANCES AT ITS CENTER OF
OF GRAVITY. IF YOU SAW THE BROOM
INTO TWO PARTS THROUGH THE CENTER
OF GRAVITY AND THEN WEIGH EACH
PART ON A SCALE, WHICH PART WILL
WEIGH MORE?

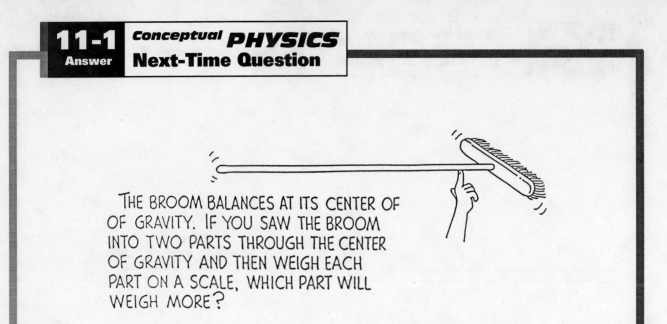

THE BROOM BALANCES AT ITS CENTER OF
OF GRAVITY. IF YOU SAW THE BROOM
INTO TWO PARTS THROUGH THE CENTER
OF GRAVITY AND THEN WEIGH EACH
PART ON A SCALE, WHICH PART WILL
WEIGH MORE?

ANSWER:

THE SHORT BROOM PART IS HEAVIER.
IT BALANCES THE LONG HANDLE JUST AS
KIDS OF UNEQUAL WEIGHTS CAN BALANCE
ON A SEESAW WHEN THE HEAVIER KID
SITS CLOSER TO THE FULCRUM. BOTH
THE BALANCED BROOM AND SEESAW
ARE EVIDENCE OF EQUAL AND OPPOSITE
TORQUES ... NOT EQUAL WEIGHTS.

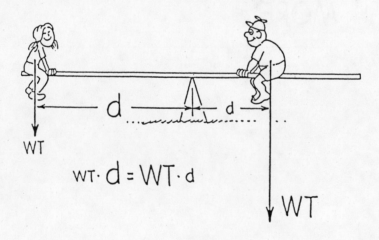

$$wt \cdot d = WT \cdot d$$

Addison-Wesley Publishing Company, Inc.

©1997

Which will roll down a hill faster, a can of regular fruit juice or a can of frozen fruit juice?

a) regular fruit juice

b) frozen fruit juice

c) depends on the relative sizes and weights of the cans

Which will roll down a hill faster, a can of regular fruit juice or a can of frozen fruit juice?

a) regular fruit juice

b) frozen fruit juice

c) depends on the relative sizes and weights of the cans

The answer is a:

The regular fruit juice has an appreciably greater acceleration down an incline than the can of frozen juice. Why? Because the regular juice is a liquid and is not made to roll with the can, as the solid juice does. Most of the liquid effectively slides down the incline inside the rolling can. The can of liquid therefore has very little rotational inertia compared to its mass. The solid juice, on the other hand, is made to rotate, giving the can more rotational inertia.

Any freely sliding object will beat any rotating object on the same incline because none of its potential energy is given to rotational kinetic energy.

©1997

THE 40-kg WOMAN STANDS AT
THE END OF A 4-METER-LONG
UNIFORM PLANK. IF THE MAXIMUM
OVERHANG FOR BALANCE IS 1 METER,
ESTIMATE THE MASS OF THE PLANK.

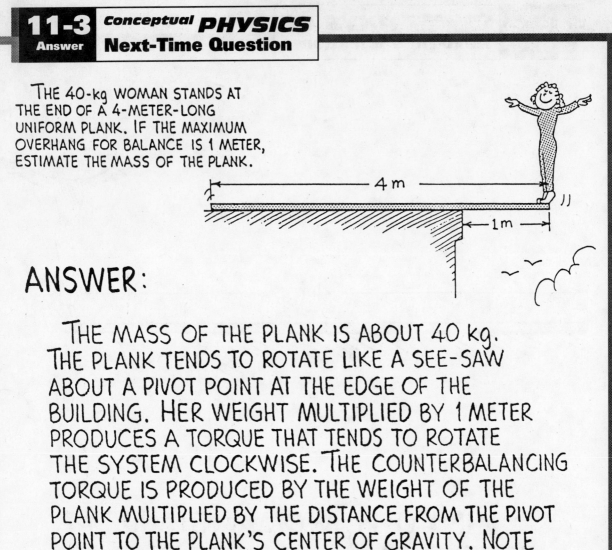

THE 40-kg WOMAN STANDS AT THE END OF A 4-METER-LONG UNIFORM PLANK. IF THE MAXIMUM OVERHANG FOR BALANCE IS 1 METER, ESTIMATE THE MASS OF THE PLANK.

4 m

1 m

ANSWER:

THE MASS OF THE PLANK IS ABOUT 40 kg. THE PLANK TENDS TO ROTATE LIKE A SEE-SAW ABOUT A PIVOT POINT AT THE EDGE OF THE BUILDING. HER WEIGHT MULTIPLIED BY 1 METER PRODUCES A TORQUE THAT TENDS TO ROTATE THE SYSTEM CLOCKWISE. THE COUNTERBALANCING TORQUE IS PRODUCED BY THE WEIGHT OF THE PLANK MULTIPLIED BY THE DISTANCE FROM THE PIVOT POINT TO THE PLANK'S CENTER OF GRAVITY. NOTE THAT THIS DISTANCE IS ALSO 1 METER. SO BOTH THE WOMAN AND THE PLANK WEIGH THE SAME. THEIR MASSES ARE EQUAL.

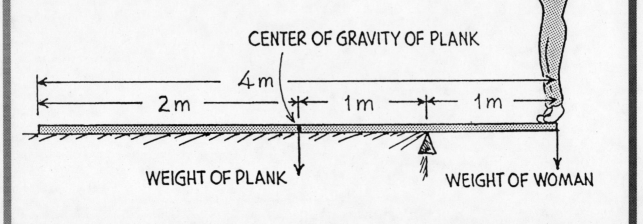

CENTER OF GRAVITY OF PLANK

4 m

2 m

1 m

1 m

WEIGHT OF PLANK

WEIGHT OF WOMAN

©1997

Suppose the gravitational force between the earth and moon was turned off and the pull replaced by the tension in a steel cable joining them. Consider the tension in such a cable, and its size. The tensile strength of a steel cable is about $5.0 \times 10^8 \, N/m^2$ (each square meter cross section can support a 5.0×10^8-newton force).

The cross-sectional area would be about that of

a) a bass guitar string.
b) a typical vertical cable that supports the George Washington Bridge (connecting NJ and NY).
c) one of the World Trade Center Towers, NY.
d) Manhattan Island, NY.
e) an area more than that of New York State.

> **You Need to Know**
> Mass of Moon = 7.4×10^{22} kg
> Mass of Earth = 6.0×10^{24} kg
> Earth-Moon distance = 3.8×10^8 m
> G (grav. constant) = 6.7×10^{-11} N·m²/kg²

Suppose the gravitational force between the earth and moon was turned off and the pull replaced by the tension in a steel cable joining them. Consider the tension in such a cable, and its size. The tensile strength of a steel cable is about $5.0 \times 10^8 \, N/m^2$ (each square meter cross section can support a 5.0×10^8-newton force).

The cross-sectional area would be about that of

a) a bass guitar string.
b) a typical vertical cable that supports the George Washington Bridge (connecting NJ and NY).
c) one of the World Trade Center Towers, NY.
d) Manhattan Island, NY.
e) an area more than that of New York State.

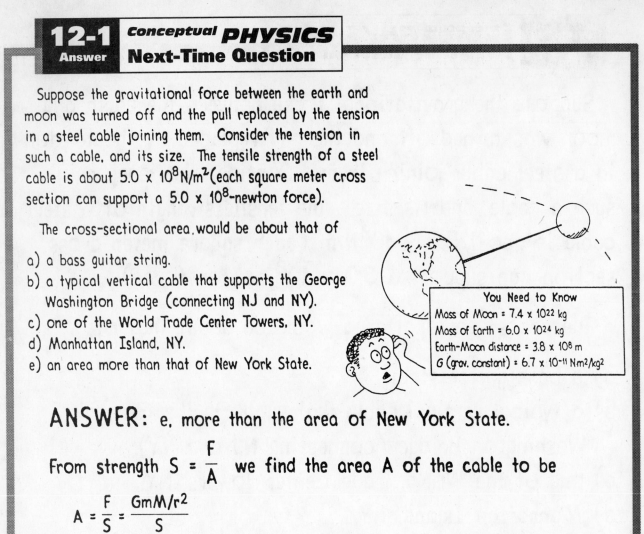

You Need to Know
Mass of Moon = 7.4×10^{22} kg
Mass of Earth = 6.0×10^{24} kg
Earth-Moon distance = 3.8×10^8 m
G (grav. constant) = 6.7×10^{-11} N·m²/kg²

ANSWER: e, more than the area of New York State.

From strength $S = \dfrac{F}{A}$ we find the area A of the cable to be

$$A = \frac{F}{S} = \frac{GmM/r^2}{S}$$

$$= \frac{(6.7 \times 10^{-11} N \cdot m^2/kg^2 \cdot 6.0 \text{wxw} 10^{24} kg \cdot 7.4 \times 10^{22} kg)/(3.8 \times 10^8 m)^2}{5.0 \times 10^8 N/m^2}$$

$$= \frac{2.0 \times 10^{20} N}{5.0 \times 10^8 N/m^2} = 4.0 \times 10^{11} \, m^2$$

That's about 400,000 square kilometers, which is more than *three times* the area of New York State! (NY has an area of 129,000 km².) Although gravitation is the weakest of the fundamental forces, we see that between great masses even long distances apart, it can be enormous.

What is the thickness of the cable? And what would be the thickness of a steel cable to replace gravitation between the Earth and the Sun?

©1997

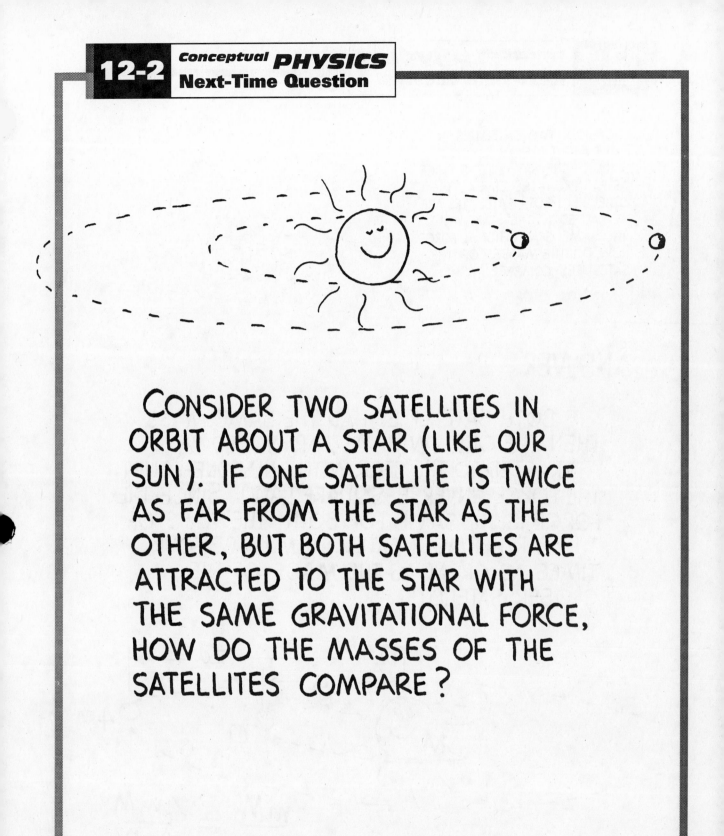

CONSIDER TWO SATELLITES IN ORBIT ABOUT A STAR (LIKE OUR SUN). IF ONE SATELLITE IS TWICE AS FAR FROM THE STAR AS THE OTHER, BUT BOTH SATELLITES ARE ATTRACTED TO THE STAR WITH THE SAME GRAVITATIONAL FORCE, HOW DO THE MASSES OF THE SATELLITES COMPARE?

CONSIDER TWO SATELLITES IN ORBIT ABOUT A STAR (LIKE OUR SUN). IF ONE SATELLITE IS TWICE AS FAR FROM THE STAR AS THE OTHER, BUT BOTH SATELLITES ARE ATTRACTED TO THE STAR WITH THE SAME GRAVITATIONAL FORCE, HOW DO THE MASSES OF THE SATELLITES COMPARE?

ANSWER:

IF BOTH SATELLITES HAD THE SAME MASS, THEN THE ONE TWICE AS FAR WOULD BE ATTRACTED TO THE STAR WITH ONLY ONE-FOURTH THE FORCE (INVERSE-SQUARE LAW). SINCE THE FORCE IS THE SAME FOR BOTH, THE MASS OF THE FARTHERMOST SATELLITE MUST BE FOUR TIMES AS GREAT AS THE MASS OF THE CLOSER SATELLITE.

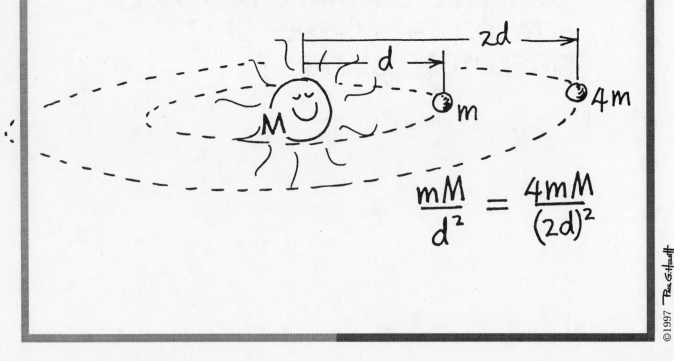

$$\frac{mM}{d^2} = \frac{4mM}{(2d)^2}$$

© 1997

Addison-Wesley Publishing Company, Inc.

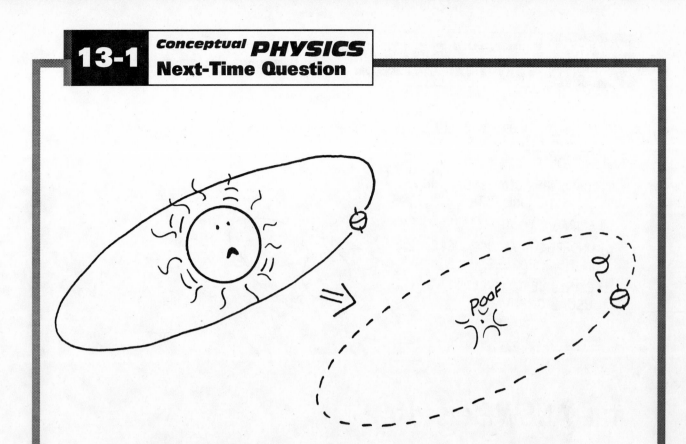

IF THE SUN SUDDENLY COLLAPSED TO BECOME A BLACK HOLE, THE EARTH WOULD

a) LEAVE THE SOLAR SYSTEM IN A STRAIGHT-LINE PATH

b) SPIRAL INTO THE BLACK HOLE

c) UNDERGO A MAJOR INCREASE IN TIDAL FORCES

d) CONTINUE TO CIRCLE IN ITS USUAL ORBIT

©1997

IF THE SUN SUDDENLY COLLAPSED
TO BECOME A BLACK HOLE, THE
EARTH WOULD

a) LEAVE THE SOLAR SYSTEM IN A
STRAIGHT-LINE PATH

b) SPIRAL INTO THE BLACK HOLE

c) UNDERGO A MAJOR INCREASE
IN TIDAL FORCES

d) CONTINUE TO CIRCLE IN ITS
USUAL ORBIT

THE ANSWER IS d:

WE CAN SEE FROM NEWTON'S EQUATION,

$$F = G\frac{mM}{d^2}$$

THAT THE INTERACTION F BETWEEN THE MASS
OF THE EARTH AND THE SUN DOESN'T CHANGE.
THIS IS BECAUSE THE MASS OF THE EARTH DOES
NOT CHANGE, THE MASS OF THE SUN DOES NOT
CHANGE EVEN THOUGH IT IS COMPRESSED, AND
THE DISTANCE FROM THE CENTERS OF THE EARTH
AND THE SUN, COLLAPSED OR NOT, DOES NOT
CHANGE. ALTHOUGH THE EARTH WOULD VERY
SOON FREEZE AND UNDERGO ENORMOUS
SURFACE CHANGES, ITS YEARLY PATH WOULD
CONTINUE AS IF THE SUN WERE ITS NORMAL SIZE.

                    Addison-Wesley Publishing Company, Inc.

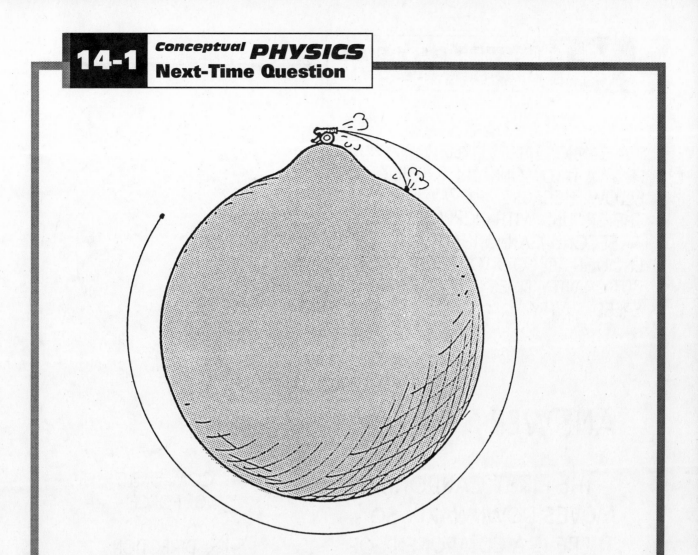

A CANNONBALL IS FIRED HORIZONTALLY
FROM A TALL MOUNTAIN TO THE GROUND
BELOW. BECAUSE OF GRAVITY, IT STRIKES
THE GROUND WITH INCREASED SPEED.
A SECOND CANNONBALL IS FIRED FAST
ENOUGH TO GO INTO CIRCULAR ORBIT---
BUT GRAVITY DOES NOT INCREASE ITS
SPEED. WHY?

A CANNONBALL IS FIRED HORIZONTALLY FROM A TALL MOUNTAIN TO THE GROUND BELOW. BECAUSE OF GRAVITY, IT STRIKES THE GROUND WITH INCREASED SPEED. A SECOND CANNONBALL IS FIRED FAST ENOUGH TO GO INTO CIRCULAR ORBIT --- BUT GRAVITY DOES NOT INCREASE ITS SPEED. WHY ?

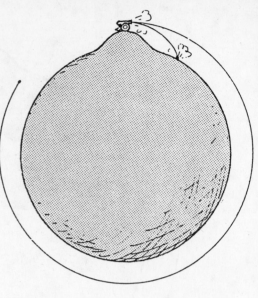

ANSWER:

THE FIRST CANNONBALL MOVES DOWNWARD, SO THERE IS A COMPONENT OF GRAVITATIONAL FORCE ALONG ITS DIRECTION OF MOTION THAT SPEEDS IT UP.

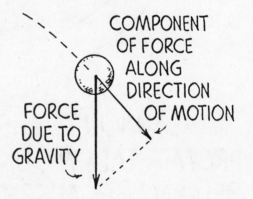

COMPONENT OF FORCE ALONG DIRECTION OF MOTION

FORCE DUE TO GRAVITY

FORCE DUE TO GRAVITY

90° BETWEEN GRAVITY AND DIRECTION OF MOTION

THE SECOND CANNONBALL MOVES PERPENDICULAR TO THE GRAVITATIONAL FORCE, WITH NO FORCE COMPONENT ALONG ITS DIRECTION OF MOTION. THAT'S WHY IT ORBITS AT CONSTANT SPEED.

©1997

Addison-Wesley Publishing Company, Inc.

CONSIDER THE VARIOUS POSITIONS OF THE SATELLITE AS IT ORBITS THE PLANET AS SHOWN. WITH RESPECT TO THE PLANET, IN WHICH POSITION DOES THE SATELLITE HAVE THE MAXIMUM

a) SPEED ?

b) VELOCITY ?

c) MOMENTUM ?

d) KINETIC ENERGY ?

e) GRAVITATIONAL POTENTIAL ENERGY ?

f) TOTAL ENERGY ?

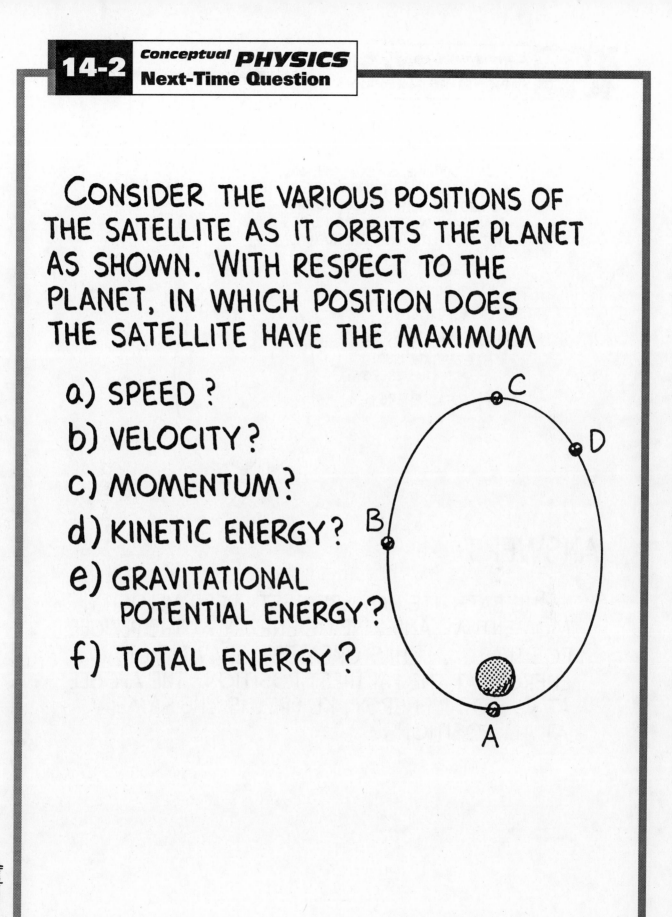

CONSIDER THE VARIOUS POSITIONS OF
THE SATELLITE AS IT ORBITS THE PLANET
AS SHOWN. WITH RESPECT TO THE
PLANET, IN WHICH POSITION DOES
THE SATELLITE HAVE THE MAXIMUM

a) SPEED?
b) VELOCITY?
c) MOMENTUM?
d) KINETIC ENERGY?
e) GRAVITATIONAL
   POTENTIAL ENERGY?
f) TOTAL ENERGY?

ANSWERS:

THE SATELLITE HAS GREATEST SPEED, VELOCITY,
MOMENTUM, AND KINETIC ENERGY AT THE PERIGEE,
POSITION **A**. IT HAS GREATEST GRAVITATIONAL
ENERGY AT THE FARTHEST POSITION, THE APOGEE
AT **C**. TOTAL ENERGY, KE + PE, IS THE SAME
AT ALL POSITIONS.

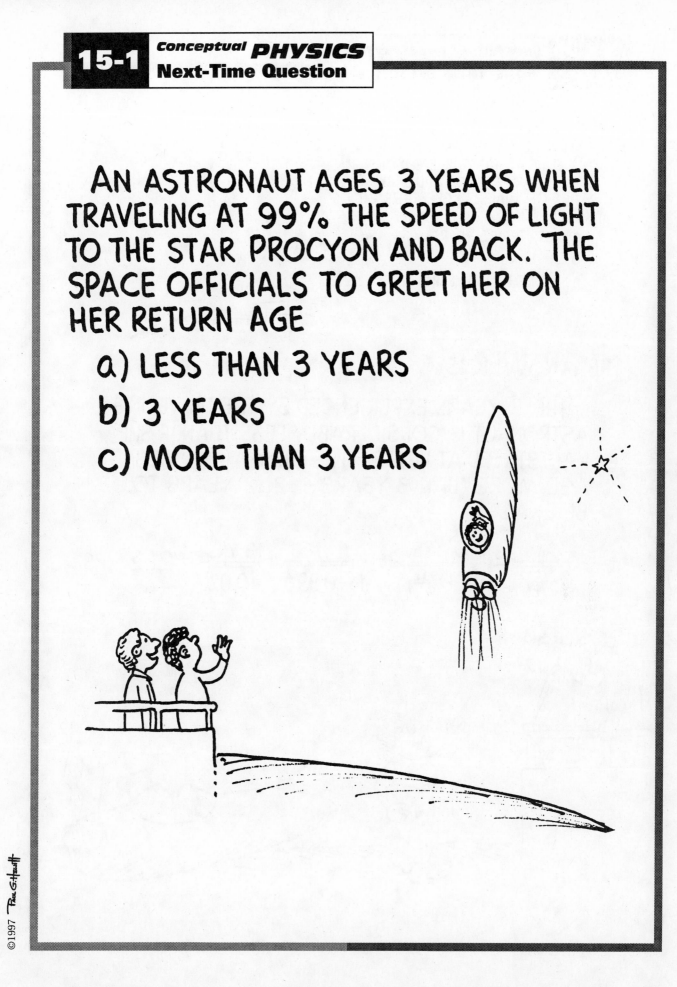

AN ASTRONAUT AGES 3 YEARS WHEN TRAVELING AT 99% THE SPEED OF LIGHT TO THE STAR PROCYON AND BACK. THE SPACE OFFICIALS TO GREET HER ON HER RETURN AGE

a) LESS THAN 3 YEARS

b) 3 YEARS

c) MORE THAN 3 YEARS

© 1997

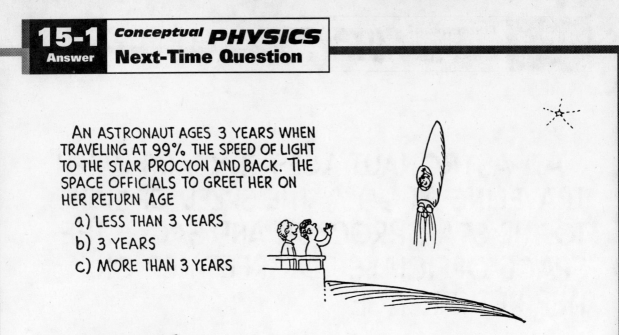

AN ASTRONAUT AGES 3 YEARS WHEN TRAVELING AT 99% THE SPEED OF LIGHT TO THE STAR PROCYON AND BACK. THE SPACE OFFICIALS TO GREET HER ON HER RETURN AGE

a) LESS THAN 3 YEARS
b) 3 YEARS
c) MORE THAN 3 YEARS

THE ANSWER IS C:

THE 3 YEARS EXPERIENCED BY THE TRAVELING ASTRONAUT IS CONSIDERABLY LESS THAN IF SHE HAD STAYED AT HOME. THE STAY-AT-HOMES AGE MORE THAN 3 YEARS --- 21.2 YEARS TO BE EXACT.

$$t = \frac{t_0}{\sqrt{1-\left(\frac{v}{c}\right)^2}} = \frac{3 \text{ YRS}}{\sqrt{1-\left(\frac{0.99c}{c}\right)^2}} = \frac{3 \text{ YRS}}{\sqrt{1-0.99^2}} = \frac{3 \text{ YRS}}{\sqrt{0.02}} = 21.2 \text{ YRS}$$

©1997

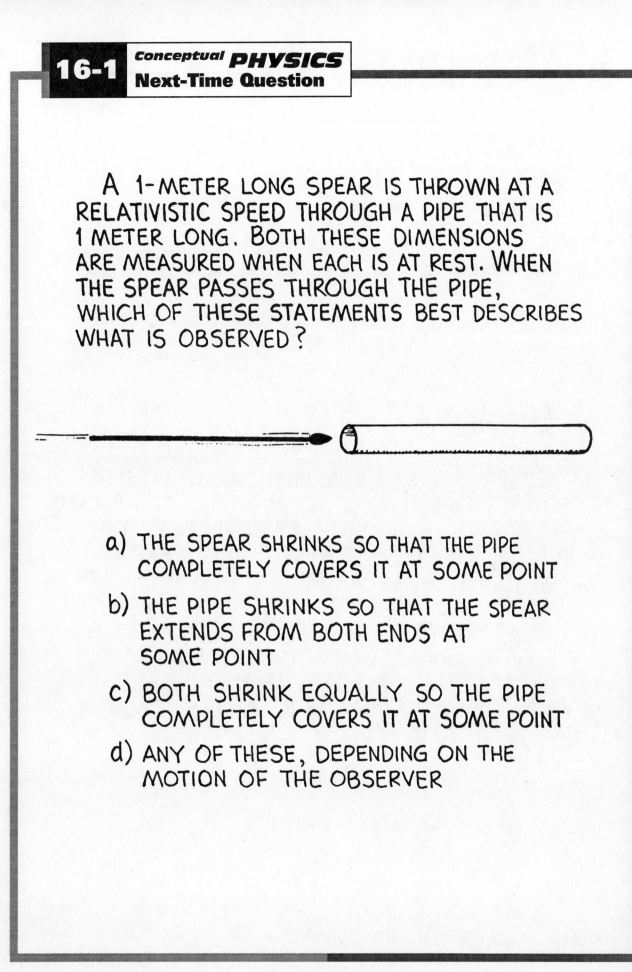

A 1-METER LONG SPEAR IS THROWN AT A RELATIVISTIC SPEED THROUGH A PIPE THAT IS 1 METER LONG. BOTH THESE DIMENSIONS ARE MEASURED WHEN EACH IS AT REST. WHEN THE SPEAR PASSES THROUGH THE PIPE, WHICH OF THESE STATEMENTS BEST DESCRIBES WHAT IS OBSERVED?

a) THE SPEAR SHRINKS SO THAT THE PIPE COMPLETELY COVERS IT AT SOME POINT

b) THE PIPE SHRINKS SO THAT THE SPEAR EXTENDS FROM BOTH ENDS AT SOME POINT

c) BOTH SHRINK EQUALLY SO THE PIPE COMPLETELY COVERS IT AT SOME POINT

d) ANY OF THESE, DEPENDING ON THE MOTION OF THE OBSERVER

©1997

A 1-METER LONG SPEAR IS THROWN AT A RELATIVISTIC SPEED THROUGH A PIPE THAT IS 1 METER LONG. BOTH THESE DIMENSIONS ARE MEASURED WHEN EACH IS AT REST. WHEN THE SPEAR PASSES THROUGH THE PIPE, WHICH OF THESE STATEMENTS BEST DESCRIBES WHAT IS OBSERVED?

a) THE SPEAR SHRINKS SO THAT THE PIPE COMPLETELY COVERS IT AT SOME POINT

b) THE PIPE SHRINKS SO THAT THE SPEAR EXTENDS FROM BOTH ENDS AT SOME POINT

c) BOTH SHRINK EQUALLY SO THE PIPE COMPLETELY COVERS IT AT SOME POINT

d) ANY OF THESE, DEPENDING ON THE MOTION OF THE OBSERVER

THE ANSWER IS d:

OBSERVE FROM A REST POSITION WITH RESPECT TO THE PIPE AND AT SOME POINT THE CONTRACTED SPEAR WILL BE COMPLETELY COVERED BY THE PIPE. OR TRAVEL ALONG WITH THE SPEAR AND YOU'LL SEE THE SPEAR AT SOME POINT EXTEND FROM THE CONTRACTED PIPE. OR MOVE BETWEEN THE SPEAR AND THE PIPE AT A CERTAIN INTERMEDIATE VELOCITY, AND SEE BOTH THE SPEAR AND THE PIPE CONTRACTED THE SAME AMOUNT. SO WHAT REALLY HAPPENS IS RELATIVE --- IT DEPENDS ON YOUR POINT OF VIEW, OR FRAME OF REFERENCE!

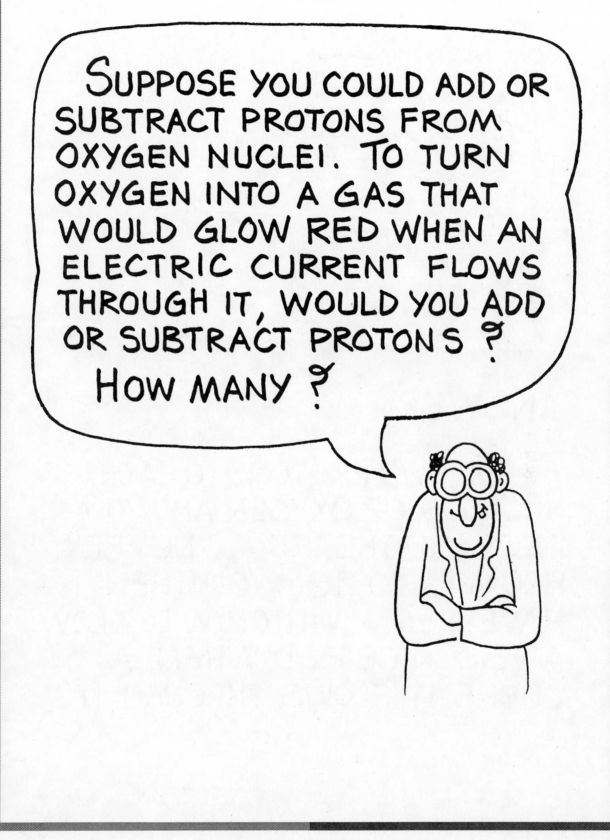

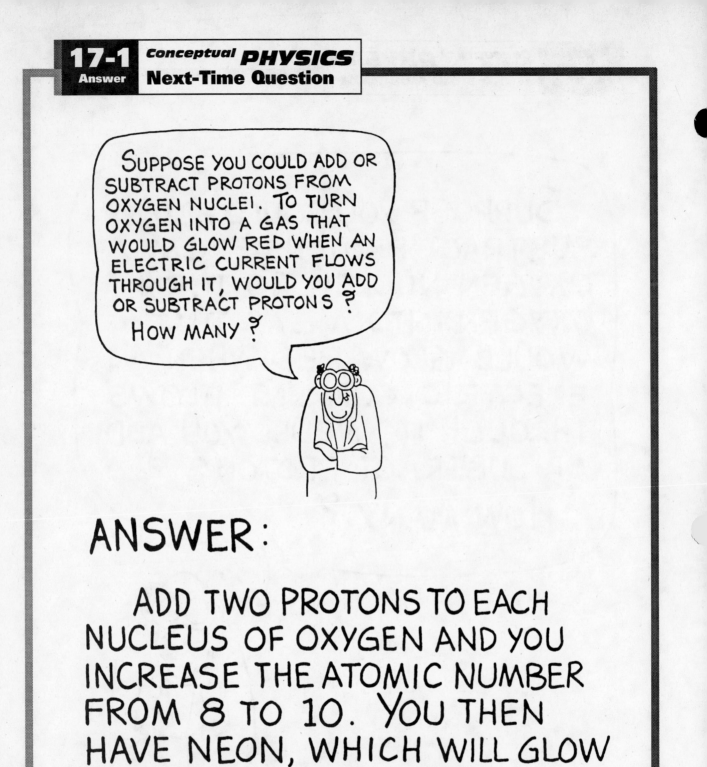

SUPPOSE YOU COULD ADD OR SUBTRACT PROTONS FROM OXYGEN NUCLEI. TO TURN OXYGEN INTO A GAS THAT WOULD GLOW RED WHEN AN ELECTRIC CURRENT FLOWS THROUGH IT, WOULD YOU ADD OR SUBTRACT PROTONS?

HOW MANY?

ANSWER:

ADD TWO PROTONS TO EACH NUCLEUS OF OXYGEN AND YOU INCREASE THE ATOMIC NUMBER FROM 8 TO 10. YOU THEN HAVE NEON, WHICH WILL GLOW A VERY NICE RED WHEN A CURRENT FLOWS THROUGH IT.

©1997

OOPS! THOSE "HARMLESS" GERMANIUM CAPSULES YOU JUST SWALLOWED MAY HAVE AN EXTRA PROTON IN EACH NUCLEUS.

IS THIS GOOD NEWS OR BAD NEWS? WHY?

Oops! Those "harmless" germanium capsules you just swallowed may have an extra proton in each nucleus.

Is this good news or bad news? Why?

ANSWER:

This is bad news, for a germanium nucleus with an additional proton is not germanium, but arsenic!

Check the periodic table ··· germanium is atomic number 32, and 33 is arsenic.

Addison-Wesley Publishing Company, Inc.

©1997

CONSIDER AN INFANT WHO WEIGHS 100 NEWTONS. DURING A YEAR SHE GROWS SO THAT EACH DIMENSION OF HER BODY INCREASES BY 5%.

HOW MUCH WILL SHE THEN WEIGH? (ASSUME HER DENSITY REMAINS UNCHANGED.)

CONSIDER AN INFANT WHO
WEIGHS 100 NEWTONS. DURING
A YEAR SHE GROWS SO THAT
EACH DIMENSION OF HER BODY
INCREASES BY 5%.

HOW MUCH WILL SHE THEN
WEIGH? (ASSUME HER DENSITY
REMAINS UNCHANGED.)

← 100 N

? N →

ANSWER:

HER WEIGHT INCREASES BY 16% AND
SHE WEIGHS 116 NEWTONS. THIS IS
BECAUSE A 5% INCREASE MEANS THAT
EACH DIMENSION OF HER BODY INCREASES
TO 1.05 WHAT IT WAS THE YEAR BEFORE.
SO THE SCALING FACTOR IS 1.05. HER
WEIGHT INCREASES IN PROPORTION TO
THE CUBE OF THIS SCALING FACTOR:

$$1.05 \times 1.05 \times 1.05 = 1.16$$

SO SHE IS 1.16 TIMES HEAVIER THAN
THE YEAR BEFORE.

©1997

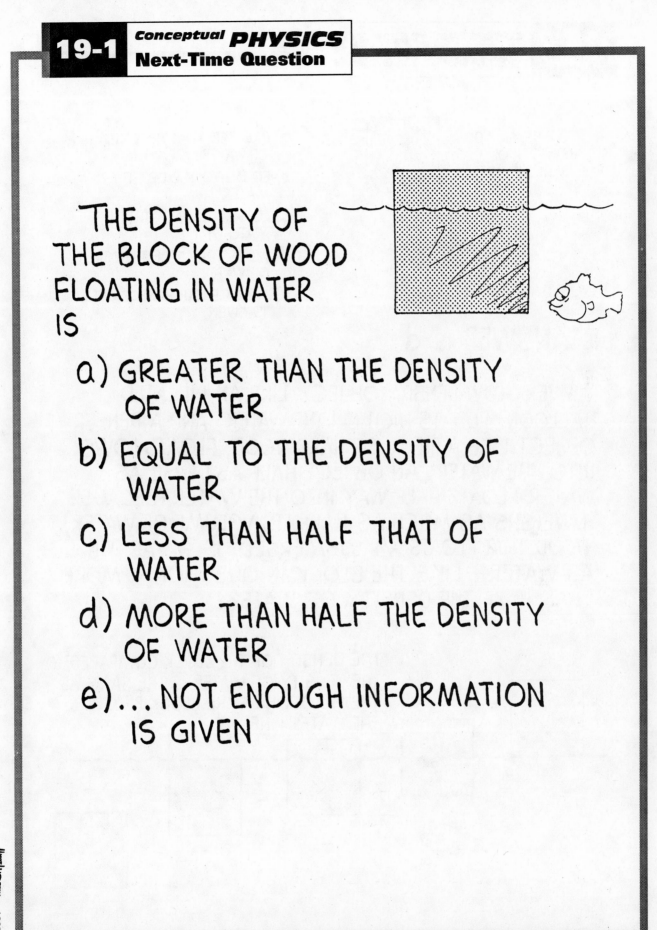

THE DENSITY OF
THE BLOCK OF WOOD
FLOATING IN WATER
IS

a) GREATER THAN THE DENSITY
OF WATER

b) EQUAL TO THE DENSITY OF
WATER

c) LESS THAN HALF THAT OF
WATER

d) MORE THAN HALF THE DENSITY
OF WATER

e)... NOT ENOUGH INFORMATION
IS GIVEN

©1997

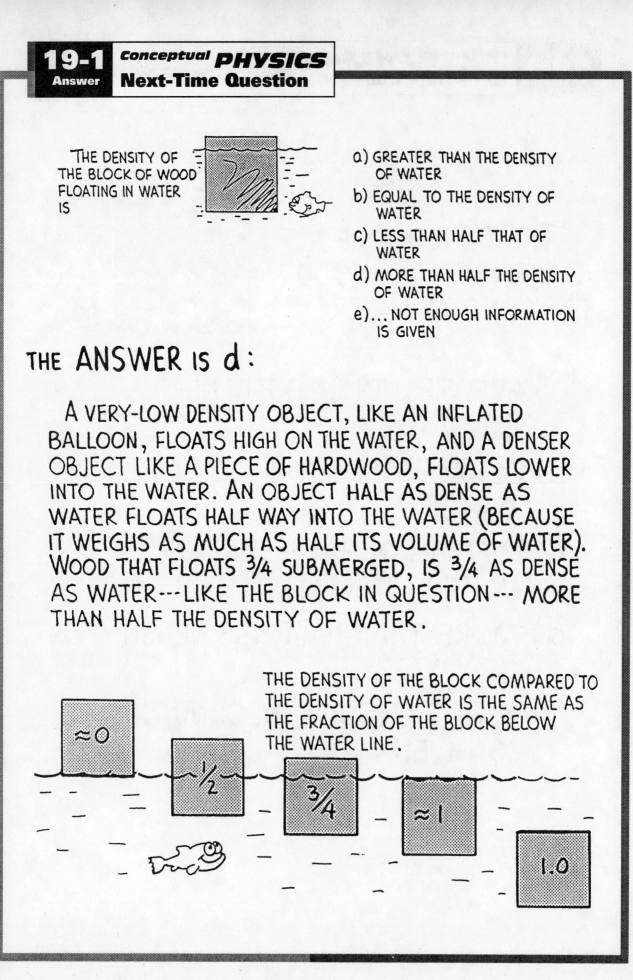

THE DENSITY OF THE BLOCK OF WOOD FLOATING IN WATER IS

a) GREATER THAN THE DENSITY OF WATER

b) EQUAL TO THE DENSITY OF WATER

c) LESS THAN HALF THAT OF WATER

d) MORE THAN HALF THE DENSITY OF WATER

e)... NOT ENOUGH INFORMATION IS GIVEN

THE ANSWER IS d:

A VERY-LOW DENSITY OBJECT, LIKE AN INFLATED BALLOON, FLOATS HIGH ON THE WATER, AND A DENSER OBJECT LIKE A PIECE OF HARDWOOD, FLOATS LOWER INTO THE WATER. AN OBJECT HALF AS DENSE AS WATER FLOATS HALF WAY INTO THE WATER (BECAUSE IT WEIGHS AS MUCH AS HALF ITS VOLUME OF WATER). WOOD THAT FLOATS 3/4 SUBMERGED, IS 3/4 AS DENSE AS WATER---LIKE THE BLOCK IN QUESTION--- MORE THAN HALF THE DENSITY OF WATER.

THE DENSITY OF THE BLOCK COMPARED TO THE DENSITY OF WATER IS THE SAME AS THE FRACTION OF THE BLOCK BELOW THE WATER LINE.

Addison-Wesley Publishing Company, Inc.

© 1997

COMPARED TO AN EMPTY SHIP,
WILL A SHIP LOADED WITH A
CARGO OF STYROFOAM FLOAT
LOWER IN WATER OR HIGHER
IN WATER?

19-2 **Answer**

Conceptual **PHYSICS**
Next-Time Question

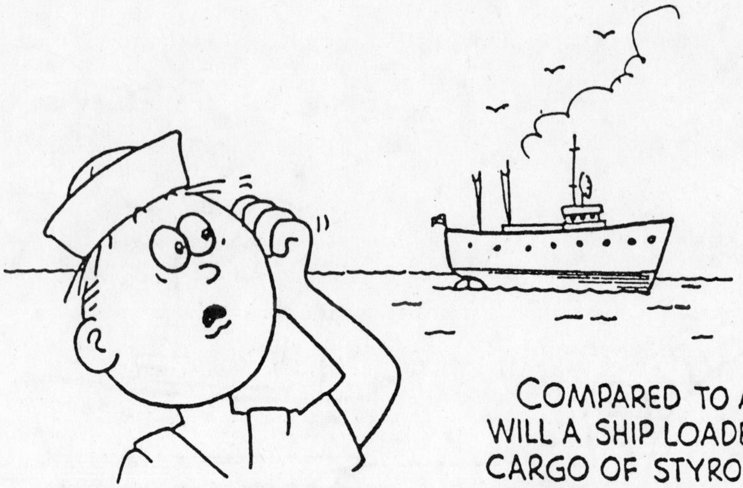

COMPARED TO AN EMPTY SHIP, WILL A SHIP LOADED WITH A CARGO OF STYROFOAM FLOAT LOWER IN WATER OR HIGHER IN WATER?

ANSWER:

THE SHIP LOADED WITH STYROFOAM WILL FLOAT LOWER IN WATER. A SHIP WILL FLOAT HIGHEST WHEN ITS WEIGHT IS LEAST--- THAT IS, WHEN IT IS EMPTY. LOADING ANY CARGO WILL INCREASE ITS WEIGHT AND MAKE IT FLOAT LOWER IN THE WATER. WHETHER THE CARGO IS A TON OF STYROFOAM OR A TON OF IRON, THE WATER DISPLACEMENT WILL BE THE SAME.

Addison-Wesley Publishing Company, Inc.

CONSIDER A BOAT LOADED WITH SCRAP IRON IN A SWIMMING POOL. IF THE IRON IS THROWN OVERBOARD INTO THE POOL, WILL THE WATER LEVEL AT THE EDGE OF THE POOL RISE, FALL, OR REMAIN UNCHANGED?

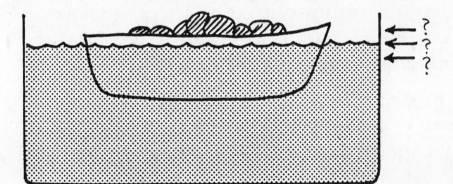

©1997

CONSIDER A BOAT LOADED WITH
SCRAP IRON IN A SWIMMING POOL.
IF THE IRON IS THROWN OVERBOARD
INTO THE POOL, WILL THE WATER
LEVEL AT THE EDGE OF THE POOL
RISE, FALL, OR REMAIN UNCHANGED?

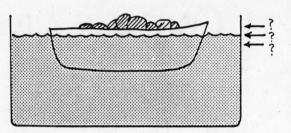

ANSWER:

THE WATER LEVEL AT THE SIDE OF THE POOL WILL
FALL, BECAUSE THE IRON WILL DISPLACE LESS
WATER SUBMERGED THAN WHEN FLOATING. WHEN
FLOATING IT DISPLACES ITS WEIGHT OF WATER
(A LOT!) --- WHEN SUBMERGED IT DISPLACES
ONLY ITS VOLUME (LESS, BECAUSE IRON IS
MORE DENSE THAN WATER).

THE MORE EXAGGERATED VIEW SHOWS
CASES FOR A VERY HEAVY BUT SMALL CANNON-
BALL ---NOTE THE DIFFERENCES IN WATER LEVELS.

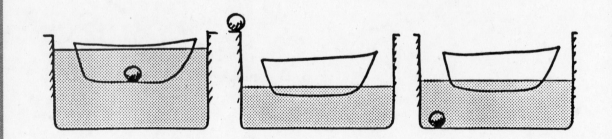

©1997

A fire truck carrying a load of fire fighters and a large tank of water is about to cross a bridge that may not support the load. The chief suggests that some of the people aboard get into the tank so the load will be less.

Is this a good idea, or a poor idea? Explain.

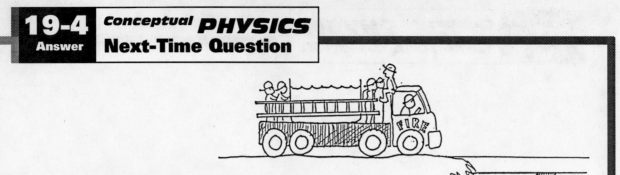

A fire truck carrying a load of fire fighters and a large tank of water is about to cross a bridge that may not support the load. The chief suggests that some of the people aboard get into the tank so the load will be less.

Is this a good idea, or a poor idea? Explain.

Answer:

This is a poor idea, because the weight of the load doesn't change when people float in the water tank. The load the bridge supports will still be the weight of the truck + people + tank + water.

The weights of the floating people are communicated to the bottom of the tank by the extra depth of water that results. So whether inside or outside the tank, their weights contribute to the load.

Weigh a pan of water on a scale. Put an apple in the water and the scale reading increases by the weight of the apple -- whether or not the apple floats.

©1997

A BLOCK OF BALSA WOOD WITH A ROCK TIED TO IT FLOATS IN WATER. WHEN THE ROCK IS ON TOP AS SHOWN, EXACTLY HALF THE BLOCK IS BELOW THE WATER LINE. WHEN THE BLOCK IS TURNED OVER SO THE ROCK IS UNDER-NEATH AND SUBMERGED, THE AMOUNT OF BLOCK BELOW THE WATER LINE IS

a) LESS THAN HALF

b) HALF

c) MORE THAN HALF

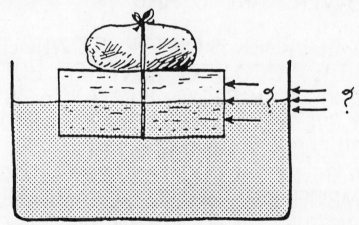

AND THE WATER LEVEL AT THE SIDE OF THE CONTAINER WILL

d) RISE

e) FALL

f) REMAIN UNCHANGED

©1997

A BLOCK OF BALSA WOOD WITH A ROCK TIED TO IT FLOATS IN WATER. WHEN THE ROCK IS ON TOP AS SHOWN, EXACTLY HALF THE BLOCK IS BELOW THE WATER LINE. WHEN THE BLOCK IS TURNED OVER SO THE ROCK IS UNDERNEATH AND SUBMERGED, THE AMOUNT OF BLOCK BELOW THE WATER LINE IS

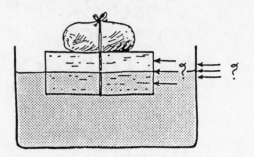

a) LESS THAN HALF
b) HALF
c) MORE THAN HALF

AND THE WATER LEVEL AT THE SIDE OF THE CONTAINER WILL

d) RISE
e) FALL
f) REMAIN UNCHANGED

THE ANSWERS ARE a AND f:

WHEN THE ROCK IS ON TOP, ITS WHOLE WEIGHT PUSHES THE WOOD INTO THE WATER. BUT WHEN THE ROCK IS SUBMERGED, BUOYANCY ON IT REDUCES ITS EFFECTIVE WEIGHT AND *LESS THAN HALF THE BLOCK* IS PULLED BENEATH THE WATER LINE. OR BY THE LAW OF FLOTATION: THE ROCK AND WOOD UNIT DISPLACES ITS COMBINED WEIGHT AND THE SAME VOLUME OF WATER WHETHER THE ROCK IS ON THE TOP OR THE BOTTOM. WHEN THE ROCK IS ON THE BOTTOM, LESS WOOD IS BELOW THE WATER LINE THAN WHEN THE ROCK IS ON THE TOP.

SINCE THE SAME VOLUME OF WATER IS DISPLACED NO MATTER HOW IT FLOATS, THE WATER LEVEL AT THE SIDE OF THE CONTAINER REMAINS *UNCHANGED*.

Addison-Wesley Publishing Company, Inc.

Compared to the mass of a dozen eggs, the mass of air in an "empty refrigerator" is

a) negligible

b) about a tenth as much

c) about the same

d) more

©1997

Compared to the mass of a dozen eggs,
the mass of air in an "empty refrigerator" is

a) negligible
b) about a tenth as much
c) about the same
d) more

Answer:

One cubic meter of air at 0°C and normal atmospheric pressure has a mass of about 1.3 kilograms. A medium-sized refrigerator has a volume of about 0.6 cubic meter and contains about 0.8 kilograms of air — more than the 0.75 kilograms of a dozen large eggs!

We don't notice the weight of air because we are submerged in air. If someone handed you a bag of water while you were submerged in water, you wouldn't notice its weight either.

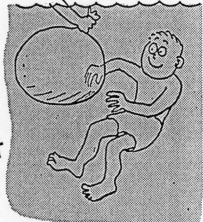

CONSIDER AN AIR-FILLED BALLOON
WEIGHTED SO THAT IT IS ON THE VERGE
OF SINKING --- THAT IS, ITS OVERALL
DENSITY JUST EQUALS THAT OF WATER.

NOW IF YOU PUSH IT BENEATH THE
SURFACE, IT WILL

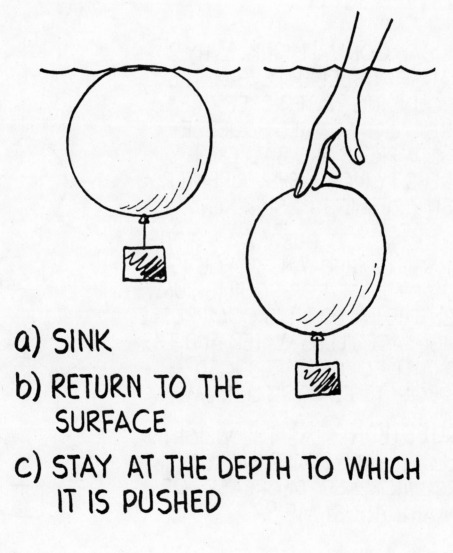

a) SINK

b) RETURN TO THE
SURFACE

c) STAY AT THE DEPTH TO WHICH
IT IS PUSHED

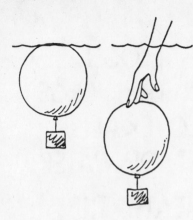

CONSIDER AN AIR-FILLED BALLOON WEIGHTED SO THAT IT IS ON THE VERGE OF SINKING --- THAT IS, ITS OVERALL DENSITY JUST EQUALS THAT OF WATER.

NOW IF YOU PUSH IT BENEATH THE SURFACE, IT WILL

a) SINK

b) RETURN TO THE SURFACE

c) STAY AT THE DEPTH TO WHICH IT IS PUSHED

THE ANSWER IS a:

THE BALLOON WILL SINK. WHY? BECAUSE AT DEEPER LEVELS THE SURROUNDING WATER PRESSURE IS GREATER AND WILL SQUEEZE AND COMPRESS THE BALLOON--- ITS DENSITY INCREASES. GREATER DENSITY RESULTS IN SINKING.

OR LOOK AT IT THIS WAY: AT THE SURFACE ITS BUOYANT FORCE IS JUST ADEQUATE FOR EQUILIBRIUM. WHEN THE BALLOON IS COMPRESSED IT DISPLACES LESS WATER AND THE BUOYANT FORCE IS REDUCED--- INADEQUATE FOR EQUILIBRIUM.

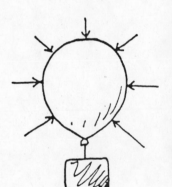

QUESTION: AS THE WEIGHTED BALLOON SINKS, WILL THE BUOYANT FORCE INCREASE, DECREASE, OR REMAIN THE SAME?

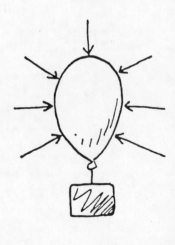

©1997

Addison-Wesley Publishing Company, Inc.

A BIRTHDAY CANDLE BURNS IN A DEEP DRINKING GLASS. WHEN THE GLASS IS WHIRLED AROUND IN A CIRCULAR PATH, SAY HELD AT ARM'S LENGTH WHILE ONE IS SPINNING LIKE AN ICE SKATER, WHICH WAY DOES THE CANDLE FLAME POINT?

©1997

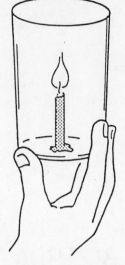

A BIRTHDAY CANDLE BURNS IN A DEEP DRINKING GLASS. WHEN THE GLASS IS WHIRLED AROUND IN A CIRCULAR PATH, SAY HELD AT ARM'S LENGTH WHILE ONE IS SPINNING LIKE AN ICE SKATER, WHICH WAY DOES THE CANDLE FLAME POINT?

ANSWER:

THE CANDLE FLAME POINTS INWARD, TOWARD THE CENTER OF THE CIRCULAR MOTION. THIS IS BECAUSE THE AIR IN THE GLASS IS MORE DENSE THAN THE FLAME AND "SLOSHES" TO THE FARTHER PART OF THE GLASS. THE GREATER AIR PRESSURE AT THE FARTHER PART OF THE INNER GLASS THEN BUOYS THE FLAME TO THE REGION OF LESSER PRESSURE---INWARD.

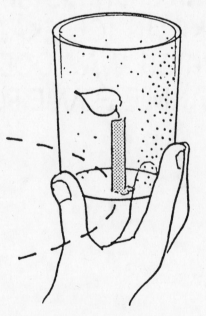

©1997

Touch the inside of a 200°C hot oven and you burn yourself. But when the 1200°C white hot sparks from a 4th-of-July-type sparkler hit your skin, you're okay. Why?

Touch the inside of a 200°C hot oven and you burn yourself. But when the 1200°C white hot sparks from a 4ᵗʰ-of-July-type sparkler hit your skin, you're okay. Why?

Answer:

Temperature is proportional to energy per molecule. How much energy depends on how many molecules. When you touch the inside surface of the oven, you're making contact with many, many molecules, and the flow of energy is a painful experience. Although the energy per molecule is much greater in the sparks of the firework, you make contact with only a relatively few molecules when a spark lands on you. The corresponding low energy transfer borders on your threshold of feeling.

High temperature at low energy is like high voltage at low energy. Both a high-temperature spark and the high voltage of a charged balloon are harmless because their energies are very small.

© 1997

A PIECE OF IRON HAS A TEMPERATURE OF 10°C. A SECOND IDENTICAL PIECE OF IRON IS TWICE AS HOT. WHAT IS THE TEMPERATURE OF THE SECOND PIECE OF IRON?

©1997

A PIECE OF IRON HAS A TEMPERATURE OF 10°C. A SECOND IDENTICAL PIECE OF IRON IS TWICE AS HOT. WHAT IS THE TEMPERATURE OF THE SECOND PIECE OF IRON?

ANSWER:

THE TWICE-AS-HOT IRON IS 293°C:

CONSIDER A STICK THAT IS 273 + 10 UNITS LONG. THIS IS LIKE A THERMOMETER THAT EXTENDS FROM ABSOLUTE ZERO (-273°C) TO 10°C. CAN YOU SEE THAT A STICK TWICE AS LONG IS 2 × 283 = 566 UNITS LONG? (OR TEMPERATURE-WISE, 566 K?)

283 C°

-273°C   0° 10°C   566 C°

-273°C   0°   293°C

SUBTRACT THE 273 PART AND YOU HAVE 566 - 273 = 293 UNITS --- LIKEWISE FOR THE TWICE-AS-HOT 10°C IRON.

©1997

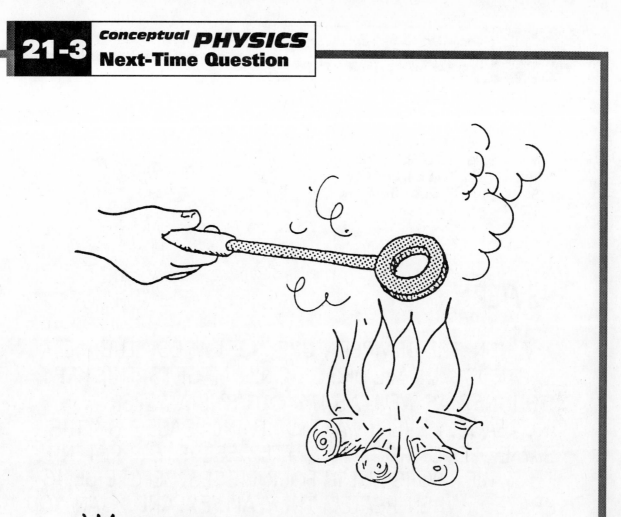

WHEN THE TEMPERATURE OF A METAL RING INCREASES, DOES THE HOLE BECOME LARGER? SMALLER? OR STAY THE SAME SIZE?

© 1997

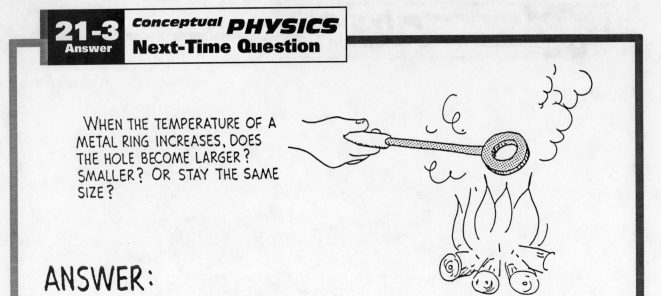

WHEN THE TEMPERATURE OF A
METAL RING INCREASES, DOES
THE HOLE BECOME LARGER?
SMALLER? OR STAY THE SAME
SIZE?

ANSWER:

WHEN THE TEMPERATURE INCREASES, THE METAL
EXPANDS---IN ALL DIRECTIONS. IT GETS THICKER;
ITS INNER AS WELL AS ITS OUTER DIAMETER
INCREASES; EVERY PART OF IT INCREASES BY THE
SAME PROPORTION. TO BETTER SEE THIS, PRETEND
THAT THE RING IS CUT IN FOUR PIECES BEFORE BEING
HEATED. WHEN HEATED THEY ALL EXPAND. CAN YOU
SEE WHEN THEY ARE REASSEMBLED THAT THE HOLE
IS LARGER?

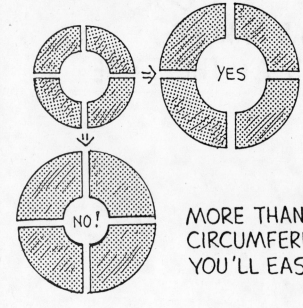

TEST THIS YOURSELF THE
NEXT TIME YOU CAN'T OPEN
THE METAL LID ON A JAR.
HEAT THE LID BY PLACING
IT ON A HOT STOVE OR
UNDER HOT WATER SO
THAT ITS TEMPERATURE
MOMENTARILY INCREASES
MORE THAN THE GLASS JAR. ITS INNER
CIRCUMFERENCE WILL INCREASE AND
YOU'LL EASILY UNSCREW THE LID!

Addison-Wesley Publishing Company, Inc.

WHEN THE TEMPERATURE OF THE PIECE OF METAL IS INCREASED AND THE METAL EXPANDS, WILL THE GAP BETWEEN THE ENDS BECOME NARROWER, OR WIDER, OR REMAIN UNCHANGED?

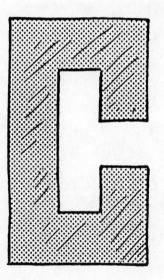

WHEN THE TEMPERATURE OF THE PIECE OF METAL IS INCREASED AND THE METAL EXPANDS, WILL THE GAP BETWEEN THE ENDS BECOME NARROWER, OR WIDER, OR REMAIN UNCHANGED?

ANSWER:

THE GAP WILL BECOME WIDER WHEN THE METAL EXPANDS. TO SEE THIS, PRETEND THE SHAPE IS COMPOSED OF LITTLE BLOCKS, EACH THE SIZE OF THE GAP. WHEN HEATED, EACH BLOCK EXPANDS THE SAME. SO IF THE METAL IS HEATED UNIFORMLY, EVERY PART EXPANDS AT THE SAME RATE ··· EVEN THE GAP.

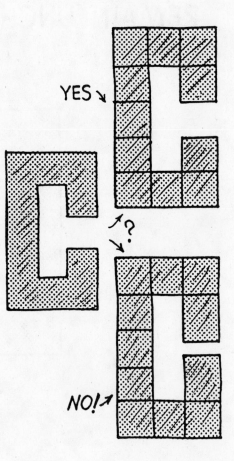

YES ↘

↗? ↘

NO! ↗

Addison-Wesley Publishing Company, Inc.

He can quickly walk barefoot across red hot coals of wood without harm because of

a) mind of matter

b) reasons that are outside mainstream physics

c) basic physics concepts

©1997 Paul G. Hewitt

He can quickly walk barefoot across red hot coals of wood without harm because of

a) mind of matter

b) reasons that are outside mainstream physics

c) basic physics concepts

The answer is c:

First of all, the coals are wood, a very poor conductor of heat. Wood is a poor conductor even when it's hot, which is why wooden handles are used on cookware. Even when the wood is red hot, its poor conductivity allows quick steps without the transfer of very much heat. High temperature and how much heat transfers are entirely different physics concepts. Secondly, if your feet are damp because of perspiration or wet surrounding grass, even less heat is transferred to your feet. Why? Two reasons: Some of the heat energy goes into evaporating the moisture that would otherwise burn you — and when the moisture turns to vapor it provides an insulating blanket. This is why you wet your finger before touching a hot clothes iron.

For mind-over-matter advocates, try walking on red hot coals of iron — ouch!

Caution: Walking on red hot coals is very dangerous and many people have accidentally burned themselves.

© 1997

Addison-Wesley Publishing Company, Inc.

A CANDLE WILL STAY
LIT INSIDE THE SPACE
SHUTTLE WHEN IT IS ON THE
LAUNCH PAD, BUT NOT WHEN
IT IS IN ORBIT. WHY?

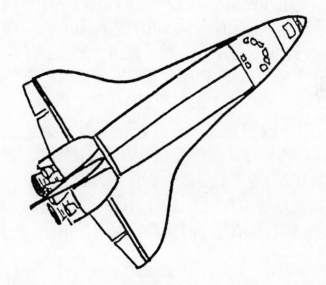

© 1997

A CANDLE WILL STAY LIT INSIDE THE SPACE SHUTTLE WHEN IT IS ON THE LAUNCH PAD, BUT NOT WHEN IT IS IN ORBIT. WHY?

ANSWER:

WHEN A CANDLE ORDINARILY BURNS, THE WARMED CARBON DIOXIDE PRODUCED IN THE FLAME RISES BY CONVECTION, AND OXYGEN COMES IN FROM BELOW TO KEEP THE PROCESS GOING. BUT WHEN IN ORBIT, THERE IS NO EFFECT OF GRAVITY INSIDE THE CABIN AND CONVECTION CANNOT OCCUR. THE WARMED EXHAUST GASES DO NOT "RISE", AND INSTEAD SUFFOCATE THE FLAME.

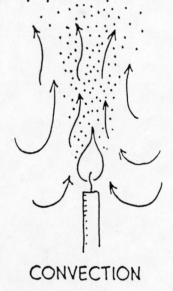

CONVECTION

NO CONVECTION

Addison-Wesley Publishing Company, Inc.

SUPPOSE IN A RESTAURANT YOUR COFFEE IS SERVED ABOUT 5 OR 10 MINUTES BEFORE YOU ARE READY FOR IT. IN ORDER THAT IT BE AS HOT AS POSSIBLE WHEN YOU DRINK IT, SHOULD YOU POUR IN THE ROOM-TEMPERATURE CREAM RIGHT AWAY OR WHEN YOU ARE READY TO DRINK THE COFFEE?

©1997

22-3
Answer

Conceptual **PHYSICS**
Next-Time Question

SUPPOSE IN A RESTAURANT YOUR
COFFEE IS SERVED ABOUT 5 OR
10 MINUTES BEFORE YOU ARE READY
FOR IT. IN ORDER THAT IT BE AS HOT
AS POSSIBLE WHEN YOU DRINK IT,
SHOULD YOU POUR IN THE ROOM-
TEMPERATURE CREAM RIGHT AWAY
OR WHEN YOU ARE READY TO
DRINK THE COFFEE?

ANSWER:

POUR THE CREAM IN RIGHT AWAY. IN SO
DOING, YOU LIGHTEN THE COLOR OF THE
COFFEE. WHEN THE COFFEE IS BLACK, IT IS
A BETTER RADIATOR AND WILL COOL FASTER
THAN WHEN IT IS LIGHTER IN COLOR. PERHAPS
YOU CAN THINK OF SOME OTHER REASONS
FOR POURING THE CREAM RIGHT AWAY.

Addison-Wesley Publishing Company, Inc.

SUPPOSE 4 GRAMS OF BOILING WATER ARE SPREAD OVER A LARGE SURFACE SO 1 GRAM RAPIDLY EVAPORATES. IF EVAPORATION TAKES 540 CALORIES FROM THE REMAINING 3 GRAMS OF WATER, AND NO OTHER HEAT TRANSFER TAKES PLACE, WHAT WILL BE THE TEMPERATURE OF THE REMAINING 3 GRAMS?

SUPPOSE 4 GRAMS OF BOILING WATER
ARE SPREAD OVER A LARGE SURFACE SO
1 GRAM RAPIDLY EVAPORATES. IF EVAPO-
RATION TAKES 540 CALORIES FROM THE
REMAINING 3 GRAMS OF WATER, AND
NO OTHER HEAT TRANSFER TAKES PLACE,
WHAT WILL BE THE TEMPERATURE OF THE
REMAINING 3 GRAMS?

ANSWER:

THE REMAINING 3 GRAMS WILL TURN TO
0°C ICE UNDER CONDITIONS WHERE ALL
540 CALORIES ARE TAKEN FROM THE REMAIN-
ING WATER (LIKE WHEN THE SURROUNDINGS
ARE BELOW FREEZING AND DON'T CONTRIBUTE
ENERGY). 540 CALORIES FROM 3 GRAMS
MEANS EACH GRAM GIVES UP 180 CALORIES.
100 CALORIES FROM A GRAM OF BOILING WATER
REDUCES ITS TEMPERATURE TO 0°C, AND
80 MORE CALORIES TAKEN AWAY TURNS IT TO
ICE. THIS IS WHY HOT WATER SO QUICKLY
TURNS TO ICE IN A FREEZING-COLD
ENVIRONMENT.

©1997

WHAT IS THE MINIMUM AMOUNT OF 100°C STEAM REQUIRED TO MELT 1 GRAM OF 0°C ICE?

ANSWER:

0.125 GRAM OF 100°C STEAM WILL PROVIDE THE 80 CALORIES REQUIRED TO MELT 1 GRAM OF ICE. THE H_2O IN THE FORM OF STEAM WILL GIVE UP 540 CALORIES PER GRAM WHEN IT CONDENSES TO BOILING WATER, AND ANOTHER 100 CALORIES PER GRAM WHEN THE WATER IS COOLED FROM 100°C TO 0°C. SO THE STEAM WILL GIVE UP A TOTAL OF 640 CALORIES PER GRAM TO THE ICE. BUT THE ICE NEEDS ONLY 80 CALORIES TO MELT. SO ONLY 80/640 GRAM (0.125 GRAM) OF STEAM WILL DO THE JOB.

24-1 *Conceptual* **PHYSICS**
Next-Time Question

The efficiency of a common incandescent lamp for converting electrical energy into heat is about

a) 5 %

b) 20 %

c) 100 %

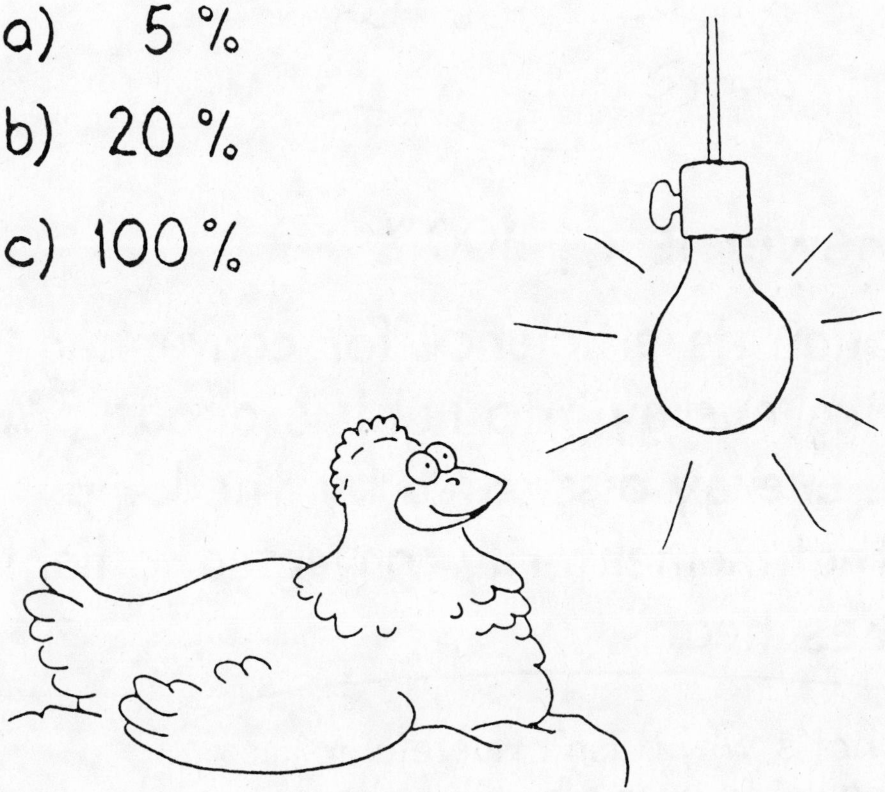

The efficiency of a common incandescent lamp for converting electrical energy into heat is about

a)   5 %

b) 20 %

c) 100 %

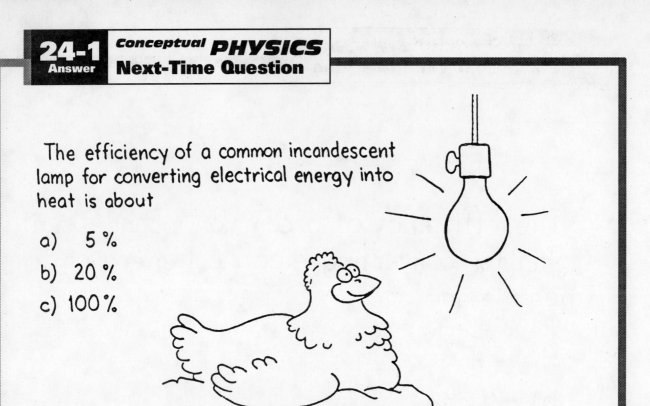

The answer is c, 100% :

Although its efficiency for converting electrical energy into light is about 5%, all the energy dissipated by the lamp, even that momentarily converted to light, becomes heat.

That's why it isn't wasteful to keep the lights on in a building that is being electrically heated!

©1997

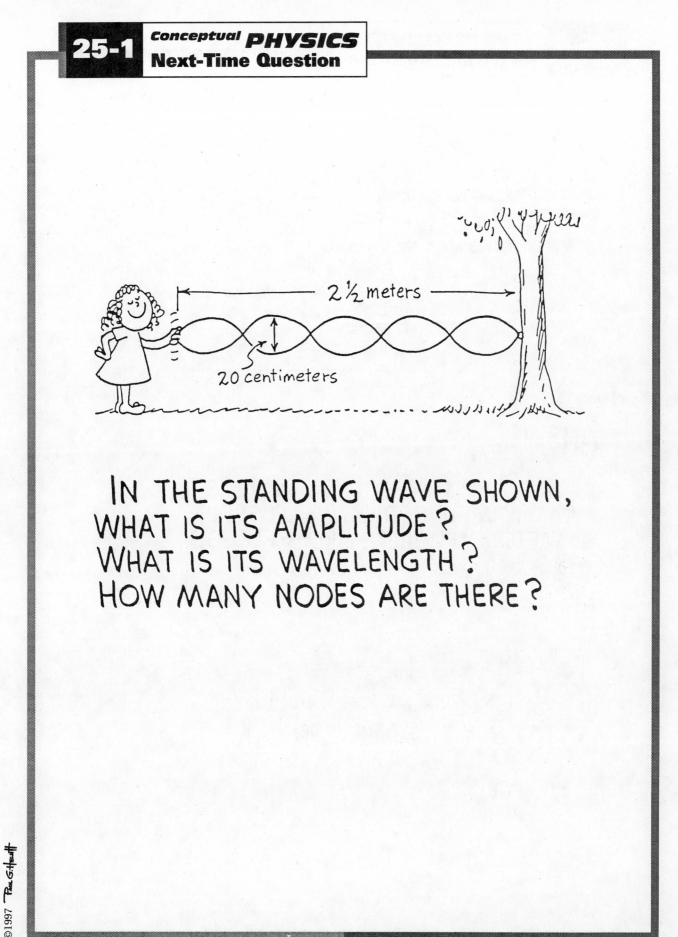

IN THE STANDING WAVE SHOWN,
WHAT IS ITS AMPLITUDE?
WHAT IS ITS WAVELENGTH?
HOW MANY NODES ARE THERE?

IN THE STANDING WAVE SHOWN,
WHAT IS ITS AMPLITUDE?
WHAT IS ITS WAVELENGTH?
HOW MANY NODES ARE THERE?

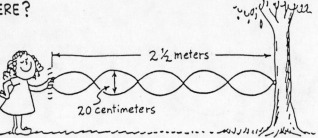

ANSWER:

THE AMPLITUDE OF THE WAVE IS
10 CENTIMETERS; THE WAVELENGTH IS
1 METER; AND THERE ARE 6 NODES.

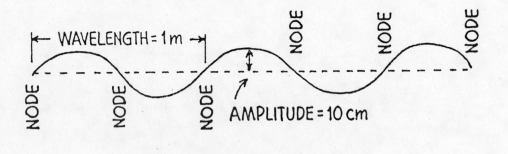

Addison-Wesley Publishing Company, Inc.

A CONICAL SHOCK WAVE IS GENERATED BY A SUPERSONIC AIRCRAFT AS SHOWN.

ESTIMATE THE SPEED OF THE CRAFT.

©1997

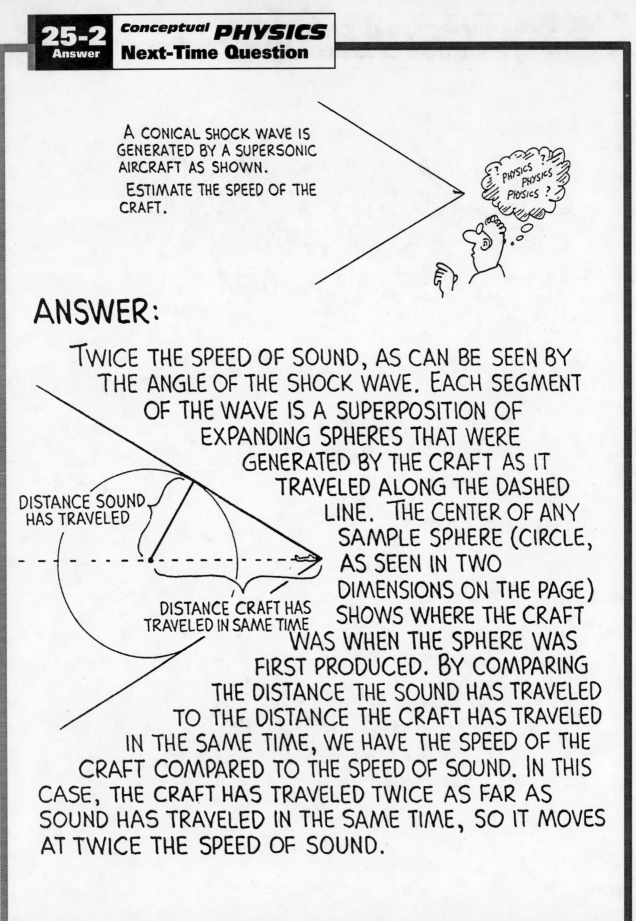

A CONICAL SHOCK WAVE IS GENERATED BY A SUPERSONIC AIRCRAFT AS SHOWN.

ESTIMATE THE SPEED OF THE CRAFT.

PHYSICS ?
PHYSICS
PHYSICS ?

ANSWER:

TWICE THE SPEED OF SOUND, AS CAN BE SEEN BY THE ANGLE OF THE SHOCK WAVE. EACH SEGMENT OF THE WAVE IS A SUPERPOSITION OF EXPANDING SPHERES THAT WERE GENERATED BY THE CRAFT AS IT TRAVELED ALONG THE DASHED LINE. THE CENTER OF ANY SAMPLE SPHERE (CIRCLE, AS SEEN IN TWO DIMENSIONS ON THE PAGE) SHOWS WHERE THE CRAFT WAS WHEN THE SPHERE WAS FIRST PRODUCED. BY COMPARING THE DISTANCE THE SOUND HAS TRAVELED TO THE DISTANCE THE CRAFT HAS TRAVELED IN THE SAME TIME, WE HAVE THE SPEED OF THE CRAFT COMPARED TO THE SPEED OF SOUND. IN THIS CASE, THE CRAFT HAS TRAVELED TWICE AS FAR AS SOUND HAS TRAVELED IN THE SAME TIME, SO IT MOVES AT TWICE THE SPEED OF SOUND.

DISTANCE SOUND HAS TRAVELED

DISTANCE CRAFT HAS TRAVELED IN SAME TIME

SUPPOSE AT A CONCERT A SINGER'S VOICE IS RADIO BROADCAST ALL THE WAY AROUND THE WORLD BEFORE REACHING THE RADIO YOU HOLD TO YOUR EAR. THIS TAKES $\frac{1}{8}$ SECOND. IF YOU'RE CLOSE, YOU HEAR HER VOICE IN AIR BEFORE YOU HEAR IT FROM THE RADIO. BUT IF YOU ARE FAR ENOUGH AWAY, BOTH SIGNALS WILL REACH YOU AT THE SAME TIME. HOW MANY METERS DISTANT MUST YOU BE FOR THIS TO OCCUR?

SUPPOSE AT A CONCERT A SINGER'S VOICE IS RADIO BROADCAST ALL THE WAY AROUND THE WORLD BEFORE REACHING THE RADIO YOU HOLD TO YOUR EAR. THIS TAKES ⅛ SECOND. IF YOU'RE CLOSE, YOU HEAR HER VOICE IN AIR BEFORE YOU HEAR IT FROM THE RADIO. BUT IF YOU ARE FAR ENOUGH AWAY, BOTH SIGNALS WILL REACH YOU AT THE SAME TIME. HOW MANY METERS DISTANT MUST YOU BE FOR THIS TO OCCUR?

ANSWER:

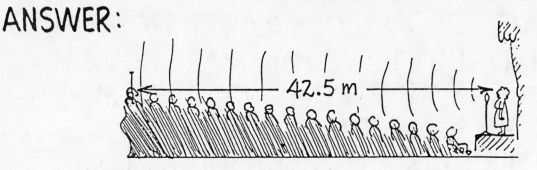

42.5 m

IF YOU SIT 42.5 METERS AWAY FROM THE SINGER, BOTH THE SOUND FROM THE RADIO THAT IS BROADCAST ALL THE WAY AROUND THE WORLD AND THAT THROUGH THE AIR WILL REACH YOU IN THE SAME ⅛ SECOND.

$$\text{DISTANCE IN AIR} = \text{SPEED OF SOUND} \times \text{TIME IN AIR}$$
$$= 340 \text{ m/s} \times ⅛ \text{ s}$$
$$= 42.5 \text{ m}$$

IF YOU SIT FARTHER BACK, YOU'LL HEAR THE RADIO SIGNAL BEFORE YOU HEAR THE SOUND SIGNAL!

Addison-Wesley Publishing Company, Inc.

IS IT CORRECT TO SAY THAT
IN EVERY CASE, WITHOUT
EXCEPTION, ANY RADIO WAVE
TRAVELS FASTER THAN ANY
SOUND WAVE?

© 1997

IS IT CORRECT TO SAY THAT IN EVERY CASE, WITHOUT EXCEPTION, ANY RADIO WAVE TRAVELS FASTER THAN ANY SOUND WAVE?

ANSWER:

YES, BECAUSE ANY RADIO WAVE TRAVELS AT THE SPEED OF LIGHT. A RADIO WAVE IS AN ELECTROMAGNETIC WAVE. SO ANY RADIO WAVE, IN A VERY REAL SENSE, IS SIMPLY A LOW-FREQUENCY LIGHT WAVE. A SOUND WAVE, ON THE OTHER HAND, IS FUNDAMENTALLY DIFFERENT. A SOUND WAVE IS A MECHANICAL DISTURBANCE PROPAGATED THROUGH A MATERIAL MEDIUM BY MATERIAL PARTICLES THAT VIBRATE AGAINST ONE ANOTHER. IN AIR, THE SPEED OF SOUND IS ABOUT 340 METERS/SECOND, ABOUT ONE-MILLIONTH THE SPEED OF A RADIO WAVE. SOUND TRAVELS FASTER IN OTHER MEDIA, BUT IN NO CASE AT THE SPEED OF LIGHT. NO SOUND WAVE CAN TRAVEL AS FAST AS LIGHT.

Addison-Wesley Publishing Company, Inc.

© 1997

Which of these lamps is emitting electromagnetic radiation?

a) Lamp A
b) Lamp B
c) Both
d) Neither

Which of these lamps is emitting electromagnetic radiation?

a) Lamp A
b) Lamp B
c) Both
d) Neither

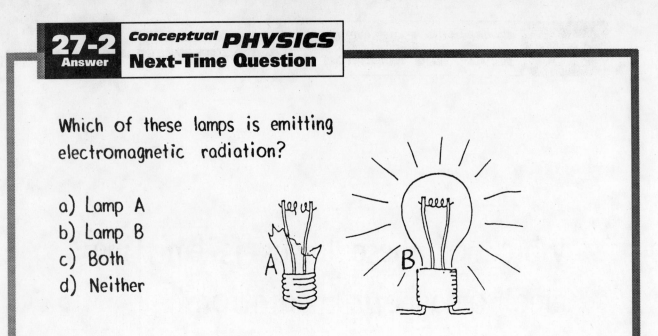

The Answer is C, both:

All bodies with any temperature at all continually emit electromagnetic waves. The frequency of these waves varies with temperature. Lamp B is hot enough to emit visible light. Lamp A is cooler, and the radiation it emits is too low in frequency to be visible -- it emits infrared waves, which aren't seen with the eye. You emit waves as well. Even in a completely dark room your waves are there. Your friends may not be able to see you, but a rattlesnake can!

If things continually emit radiation, why don't they cool to absolute zero?

©1997 Paul G. Hewitt

Addison-Wesley Publishing Company, Inc.

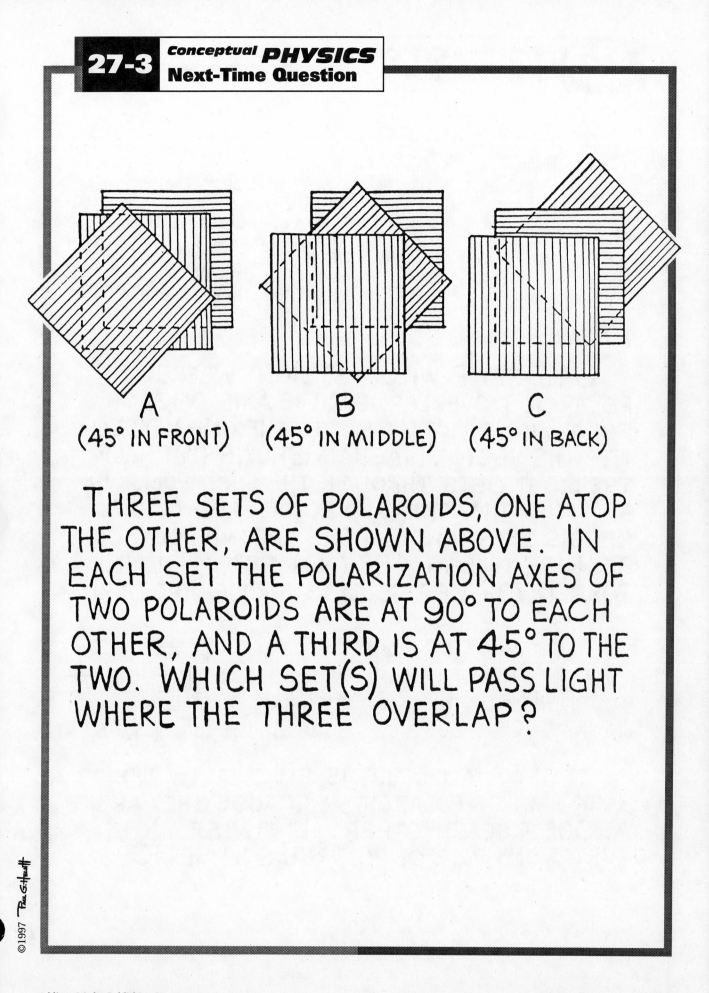

A
(45° IN FRONT)

B
(45° IN MIDDLE)

C
(45° IN BACK)

THREE SETS OF POLAROIDS, ONE ATOP THE OTHER, ARE SHOWN ABOVE. IN EACH SET THE POLARIZATION AXES OF TWO POLAROIDS ARE AT 90° TO EACH OTHER, AND A THIRD IS AT 45° TO THE TWO. WHICH SET(S) WILL PASS LIGHT WHERE THE THREE OVERLAP?

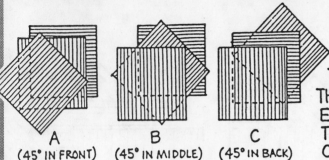

A
(45° IN FRONT)

B
(45° IN MIDDLE)

C
(45° IN BACK)

THREE SETS OF POLAROIDS, ONE ATOP THE OTHER, ARE SHOWN ABOVE. IN EACH SET THE POLARIZATION AXES OF TWO POLAROIDS ARE AT 90° TO EACH OTHER, AND A THIRD IS AT 45° TO THE TWO. WHICH SET(S) WILL PASS LIGHT WHERE THE THREE OVERLAP?

ANSWER:

ONLY SET B WILL PASS LIGHT WHERE ALL POLAROIDS OVERLAP, FOR THE AXIS OF EACH POLAROID IS NOT AT 90° TO THE ONE NEXT TO IT. THE VECTOR DIAGRAM SHOWS THAT HALF THE LIGHT GETS THROUGH THE FIRST POLAROID, SHOWN BY THE VERTICAL VECTOR, AND 0.707 OF THIS GETS THROUGH THE SECOND POLAROID BECAUSE IT IS AT 45° (NOT 90°!), AND IN TURN 0.707 OF THIS GETS THROUGH THE THIRD.

100 %   50%   (0.707)50%   (0.707)(0.707)50%

IN SET A ALL LIGHT IS BLOCKED BY THE BACK PAIR OF POLAROIDS BECAUSE THEY ARE AT 90° TO EACH OTHER. LIKEWISE WITH THE FRONT PAIR OF POLAROIDS IN SET C.

Addison-Wesley Publishing Company, Inc.

28-1 Conceptual *PHYSICS* Next-Time Question

When three colored lamps, red, blue and green, illuminate a physics instructor in front of a white screen in a dark room, three slightly-overlapping shadows appear. Specify the colors in regions 1 through 6.

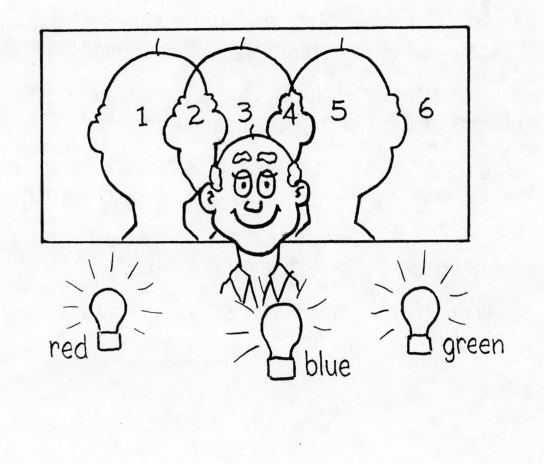

When three colored lamps, red, blue and green, illuminate a physics instructor in front of a white screen in a dark room, three slightly-overlapping shadows appear. Specify the colors in regions 1 through 6.

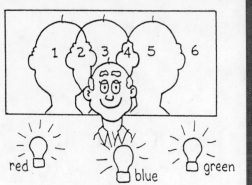

Answers:

Region 1 (shadow of the green lamp) is magenta--- illuminated by red and blue light.

Region 2 (shadow of over-lapped blue and green lamps) is red---illuminated by only red light.

Region 3 (shadow of the blue lamp) is yellow--- illuminated by red and green light.

Region 4 (shadow of over-lapped red and blue lamps) is green---illuminated by only green light.

Region 5 (shadow of the red lamp) is cyan--- illuminated by blue and green light.

Region 6 (non-shadowed screen) is white--- the addition of red, green and blue light.

Like this

©1997

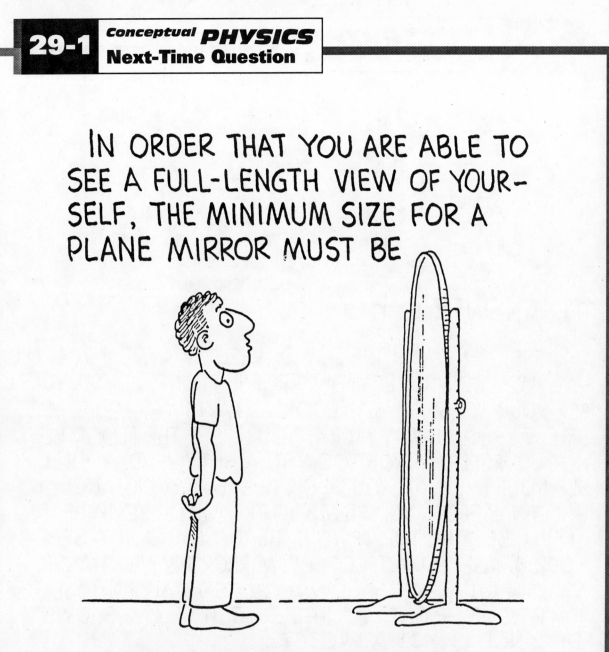

IN ORDER THAT YOU ARE ABLE TO SEE A FULL-LENGTH VIEW OF YOUR-SELF, THE MINIMUM SIZE FOR A PLANE MIRROR MUST BE

a) ONE-QUARTER YOUR HEIGHT

b) ONE-HALF YOUR HEIGHT

c) THREE-QUARTERS YOUR HEIGHT

d) YOUR FULL HEIGHT

e) ... DEPENDS ON YOUR DISTANCE

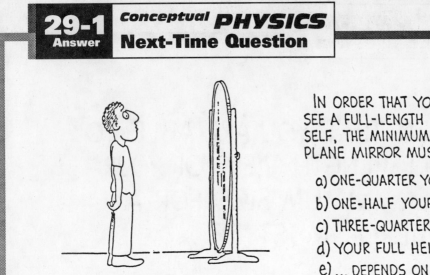

IN ORDER THAT YOU ARE ABLE TO
SEE A FULL-LENGTH VIEW OF YOUR-
SELF, THE MINIMUM SIZE FOR A
PLANE MIRROR MUST BE

a) ONE-QUARTER YOUR HEIGHT

b) ONE-HALF YOUR HEIGHT

c) THREE-QUARTERS YOUR HEIGHT

d) YOUR FULL HEIGHT

e) ... DEPENDS ON YOUR DISTANCE

THE **ANSWER** IS **b**:

CONSISTENT WITH THE LAW OF REFLECTION, IF YOU LOOK
HALF WAY DOWN A PLANE MIRROR IN FRONT OF YOU, YOU'LL
SEE YOUR TOES. IF YOU LOOK AT PARTS OF THE MIRROR
BELOW THE HALF-WAY MARK, YOU'LL SEE THE FLOOR BUT
NOT YOURSELF. IF YOU LOOK STRAIGHT AHEAD, YOU'LL
SEE YOUR EYES. IF YOU LOOK ABOVE AT A DISTANCE
HALF WAY FROM YOUR EYES TO THE TOP OF YOUR HEAD,
YOU'LL SEE THE TOP OF YOUR HEAD. YOU DON'T SEE
YOUR IMAGE IN PARTS OF THE MIRROR ABOVE. HALF
WAY UP ; HALF WAY DOWN --- THATS A MIRROR ONE-
HALF YOUR HEIGHT. AS THE SKETCH BELOW SHOWS,
DISTANCE IS NOT A FACTOR.

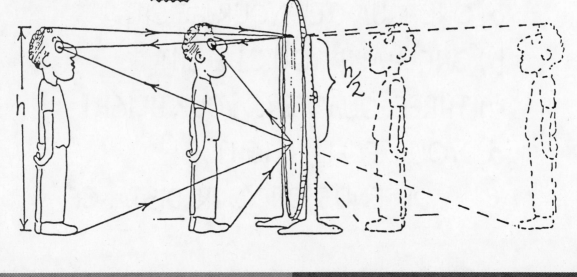

Addison-Wesley Publishing Company, Inc.

©1997

TO SEE MORE OF HER HEAD IN THE MIRROR, SHE

    a) SHOULD HOLD THE MIRROR CLOSER

    b) SHOULD HOLD THE MIRROR FARTHER AWAY

    c) NEEDS A BIGGER MIRROR

©1997

To SEE MORE OF HER HEAD IN
THE MIRROR, SHE

   a) SHOULD HOLD THE MIRROR
      CLOSER

   b) SHOULD HOLD THE MIRROR
      FARTHER AWAY

   c) NEEDS A BIGGER MIRROR

THE ANSWER IS C:

IF SHE HOLDS THE MIRROR CLOSER, HER
IMAGE APPEARS BIGGER, BUT SO DOES THE
MIRROR. IF SHE HOLDS THE MIRROR FARTHER
AWAY, BOTH HER IMAGE
AND THE MIRROR ARE
PROPORTIONALLY REDUCED.
AS THE RAY DIAGRAMS
SHOW, SHE SEES THE SAME
PROPORTION OF HER
FACE AT ANY DISTANCE.
TRY THIS YOURSELF
AND SEE! AND IF YOU
CAN NOT SEE YOUR
FULL FACE, YOU NEED
A BIGGER MIRROR.
HOW BIG? AT LEAST
HALF THE SIZE OF
YOUR FACE.

©1997

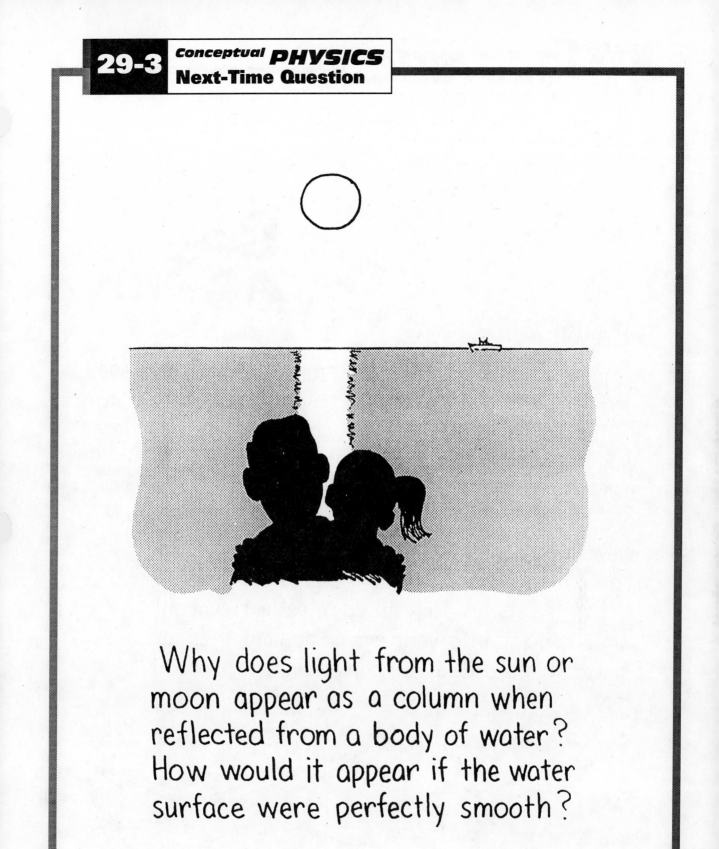

Why does light from the sun or moon appear as a column when reflected from a body of water? How would it appear if the water surface were perfectly smooth?

Why does light from the sun or moon appear as a column when reflected from a body of water? How would it appear if the water surface were perfectly smooth?

Answer :

If the water were perfectly smooth, a mirror image of the round sun or moon would be seen in the water. If the water were slightly rough, the image would be wavy. If the water were a bit more rough, little glimmers of the sun or moon would be seen above and below the main image. This is because the water waves act like an assemblage of small flat mirrors. For rougher waves, there is a greater variety of mirror facets properly tilted to reflect sunlight or moonlight into your eye. The light then appears smeared into a long vertical column.

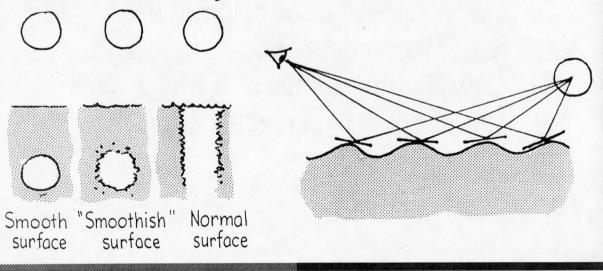

Smooth
surface
"Smoothish"
surface
Normal
surface

Addison-Wesley Publishing Company, Inc.

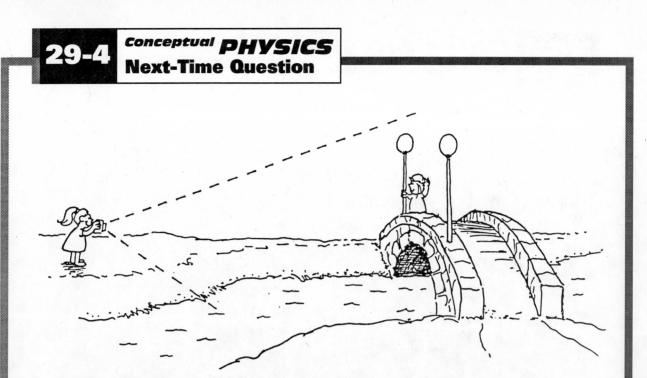

She takes a photograph of her friend standing on the bridge as shown. Which of the two sketches more accurately shows the photograph of the bridge and its reflection?

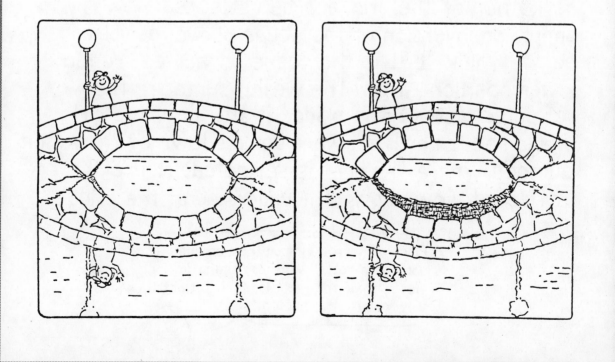

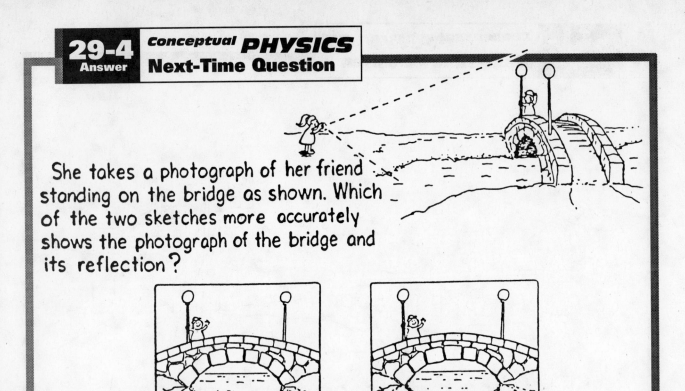

She takes a photograph of her friend standing on the bridge as shown. Which of the two sketches more accurately shows the photograph of the bridge and its reflection?

Answer:

The sketch on the right shows a more accurate reflection of the bridge. The reflected view is not simply an inversion of the scene above, as some people think, but is the scene as viewed from a lower position -- from the water surface. The reflected view of the bridge is the view the girl would see if her head were upside down at the water surface where the light is reflected. Hence the reflected view shows the underside of the bridge.

Place a mirror flat on the floor between you and a table. Whereas the ordinary view shows the table top, the reflected view shows the bottom.

Addison-Wesley Publishing Company, Inc.

©1997

A COIN LIES SUBMERGED AT THE BOTTOM OF A PAN OF WATER. DOES REFRACTION OF LIGHT FROM THE COIN MAKE IT APPEAR DEEPER, OR MAKE IT APPEAR SHALLOWER THAN IT REALLY IS?

©1997

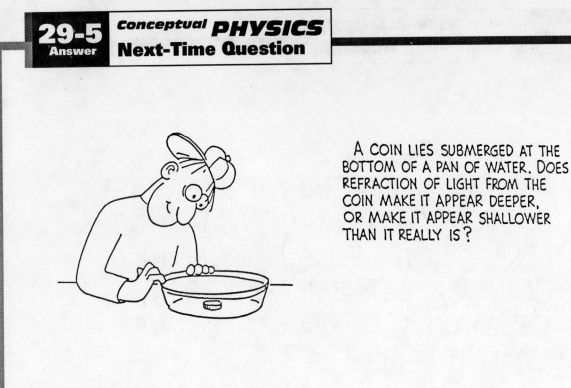

A COIN LIES SUBMERGED AT THE BOTTOM OF A PAN OF WATER. DOES REFRACTION OF LIGHT FROM THE COIN MAKE IT APPEAR DEEPER, OR MAKE IT APPEAR SHALLOWER THAN IT REALLY IS?

ANSWER:

THE COIN APPEARS SHALLOWER THAN IT REALLY IS. TO LOCATE THE IMAGE, DRAW AT LEAST TWO DIFFERENT RAYS FROM THE OBJECT AND NOTE WHERE THEY APPEAR TO MEET IF EXTENDED BACK- WARDS. THAT'S WHERE THE IMAGE IS SEEN. IF YOU LOOK STRAIGHT DOWN, THE IMAGE IS ONLY ¾ THE ACTUAL DEPTH.

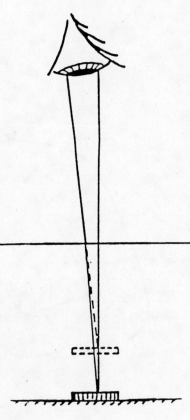

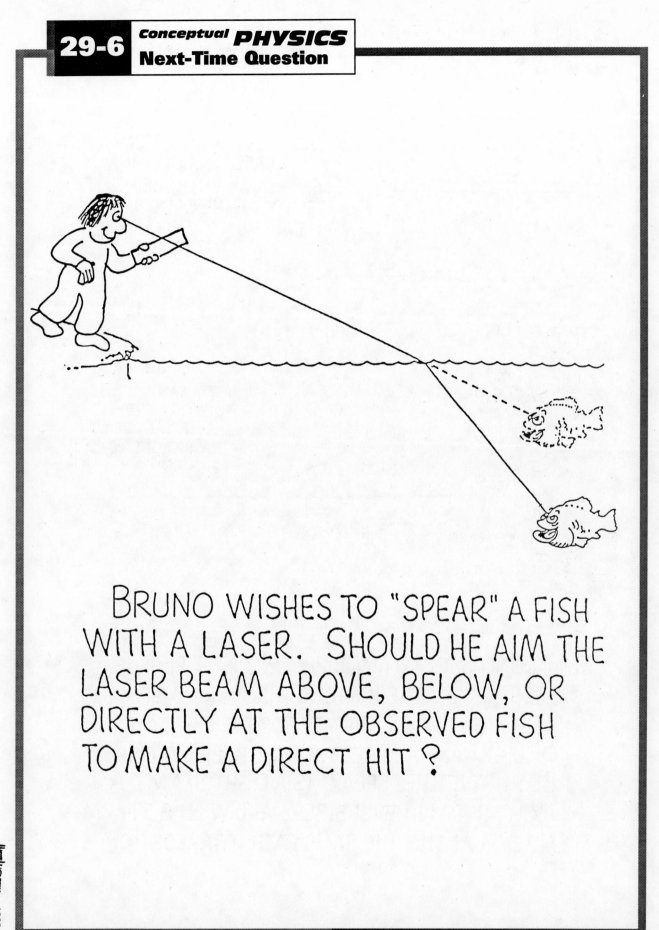

BRUNO WISHES TO "SPEAR" A FISH
WITH A LASER. SHOULD HE AIM THE
LASER BEAM ABOVE, BELOW, OR
DIRECTLY AT THE OBSERVED FISH
TO MAKE A DIRECT HIT ?

©1997

BRUNO WISHES TO "SPEAR" A FISH WITH A LASER. SHOULD HE AIM THE LASER BEAM ABOVE, BELOW, OR DIRECTLY AT THE OBSERVED FISH TO MAKE A DIRECT HIT ?

ANSWER:

LINE OF SIGHT

AIM A LASER ALONG LINE OF SIGHT --- THEN IT WILL REFRACT DOWNWARD TOWARD FISH HERE

AIM A SPEAR BELOW LINE OF SIGHT

A

B

BRUNO SHOULD AIM DIRECTLY AT THE FISH HE SEES. IF HE WERE INSTEAD THROWING A SPEAR, HE'D HAVE TO COMPENSATE FOR THE REFRACTION OF LIGHT AND AIM BELOW THE OBSERVED FISH. BUT NOT IF THE "SPEAR" IS A LIGHT BEAM! A LIGHT PATH IS REVERSIBLE, AND WILL GO FROM A TO B ALONG THE SAME PATH IT TAKES FROM B TO A.

©1997

Suppose you want to send a beam of laser light to a space station above the atmosphere and just above the horizon. You should aim your laser

a) slightly higher than

b) slightly lower than

c) directly along

the line of sight to the space station.

Suppose you want to send a beam of laser light to a space station above the atmosphere and just above the horizon. You should aim your laser

a) slightly higher than

b) slightly lower than

c) directly along

the line of sight to the space station.

The answer is C:

To send light to the space station, make no corrections and simply aim at the station you see. All deviations due to atmospheric refraction in your line of sight will be the same for your laser beam -- principle of reciprocity.

How about if the laser is red and the space station blue?

Addison-Wesley Publishing Company, Inc.

©1997

A LUNAR ECLIPSE OCCURS WHEN THE MOON PASSES INTO THE EARTH'S SHADOW. INSTEAD OF BEING COMPLETELY DARK, THE MOON APPEARS A DEEP RED. WHAT DOES THIS REDDISH COLOR HAVE TO DO WITH THE SUNSETS ALL OVER THE WORLD?

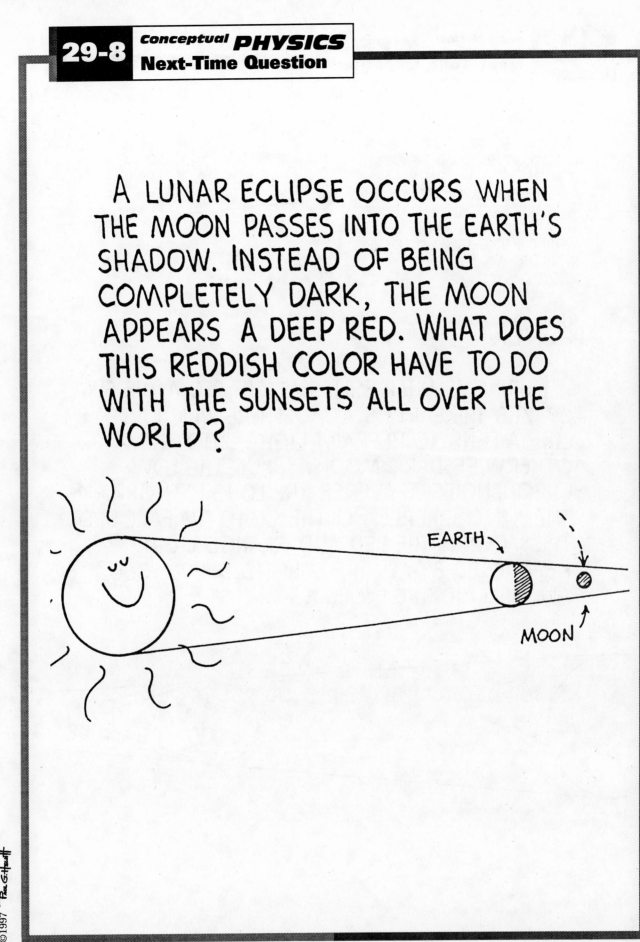

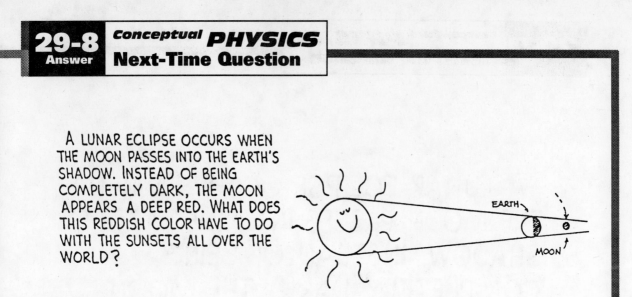

A LUNAR ECLIPSE OCCURS WHEN
THE MOON PASSES INTO THE EARTH'S
SHADOW. INSTEAD OF BEING
COMPLETELY DARK, THE MOON
APPEARS A DEEP RED. WHAT DOES
THIS REDDISH COLOR HAVE TO DO
WITH THE SUNSETS ALL OVER THE
WORLD?

ANSWER:

DURING A LUNAR ECLIPSE, LIGHT FROM THE SUN
GRAZES THE EARTH'S ATMOSPHERE WHICH ACTS
LIKE A LENS TO REFRACT LIGHT ONTO THE
OTHERWISE DARK MOON. ONLY THE LOW
FREQUENCIES TRAVERSE THE LONG PATH THROUGH
THE ATMOSPHERE. SO THE LIGHT TO FALL UPON
THE MOON IS THE RED AND ORANGE LIGHT
REFRACTED BY ALL THE SUNSETS, A FULL 360°,
ALL AROUND THE WORLD.

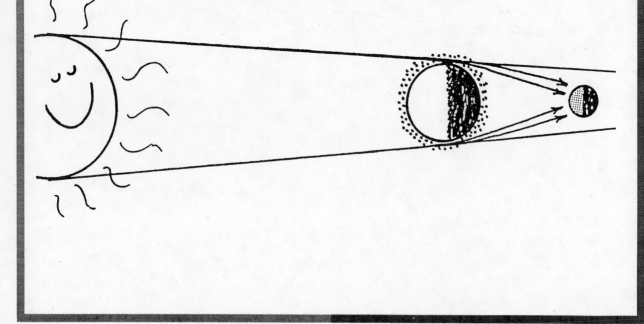

The photographer wishes to photograph the rainbow but is disappointed to find the camera's angle of view is not wide enough to see the whole rainbow. To get the whole rainbow, she would be better off if she were

a) closer to the rainbow

b) farther from the rainbow

c) ... neither, for she'd get the same portion of bow in either case

The photographer wishes to photograph the rainbow but is disappointed to find the camera's angle of view is not wide enough to see the whole rainbow. To get the whole rainbow, she would be better off if she were

a) closer to the rainbow

b) farther from the rainbow

c) ... neither, for she'd get the same portion of bow in either case

The answer is c:

Any full circle rainbow, near or far, subtends an angle of 84°. So to photograph a full rainbow, whether a very close one produced by a hand-held garden hose or one miles away, the camera's field of view must be at least 84° — a very wide-angle lens. It is the angle of view, not the distance, that matters.

All rainbows, by the way, are completely round, as can be seen from a high-flying helicopter. Viewed from below, however, the ground gets in the way. To photograph a full-circle rainbow from a helicopter, the 84° field of view must be vertical as well as horizontal. Has anyone successfully taken a photograph of a full-circle rainbow?

84°

near

far

A PERSON WHO SEES MORE CLEARLY
UNDER WATER THAN IN AIR WITHOUT
EYEGLASSES IS

a) NEARSIGHTED

b) FARSIGHTED

c) NEITHER

A PERSON WHO SEES MORE CLEARLY
UNDER WATER THAN IN AIR WITHOUT
EYEGLASSES IS
 a) NEARSIGHTED
 b) FARSIGHTED
 c) NEITHER

ANSWER:

NEARSIGHTED. THE SPEED OF LIGHT IN WATER IS
LESS THAN IN AIR, SO THE CHANGE IN SPEED IS LESS
AS LIGHT GOES FROM WATER TO YOUR EYE. LESS
REFRACTION OCCURS. THIS MAKES ALL PEOPLE
MORE FARSIGHTED UNDER WATER, WHICH IS
ADVANTAGEOUS IF YOU'RE NEARSIGHTED. IF YOU'RE
VERY NEARSIGHTED, THE IMAGE MAY FALL ON YOUR
RETINA AND YOU'LL SEE AS CLEARLY UNDER WATER
AS A PERSON WITH NORMAL VISION WHO WEARS
AN AIR-ENCLOSED MASK.

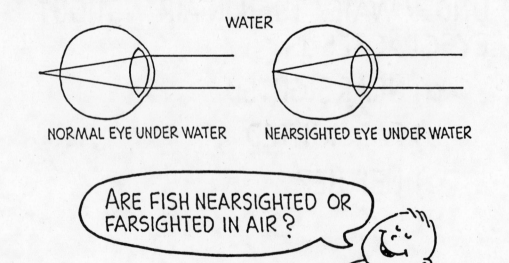

WATER

NORMAL EYE UNDER WATER   NEARSIGHTED EYE UNDER WATER

ARE FISH NEARSIGHTED OR
FARSIGHTED IN AIR?

©1997

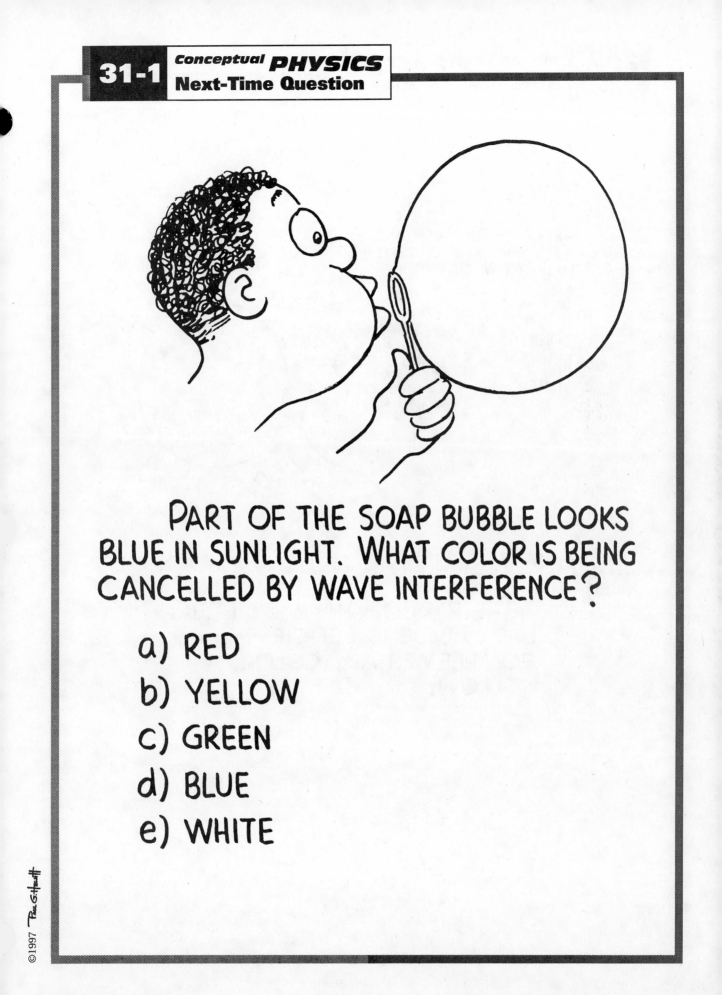

PART OF THE SOAP BUBBLE LOOKS BLUE IN SUNLIGHT. WHAT COLOR IS BEING CANCELLED BY WAVE INTERFERENCE?

a) RED
b) YELLOW
c) GREEN
d) BLUE
e) WHITE

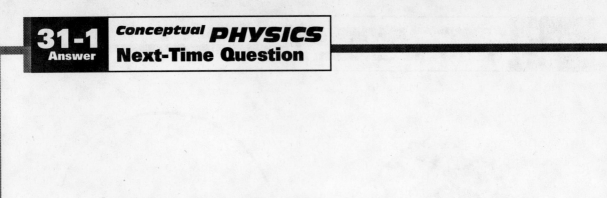

PART OF THE SOAP BUBBLE LOOKS
BLUE IN SUNLIGHT. WHAT COLOR IS BEING
CANCELLED BY WAVE INTERFERENCE?

a) RED
b) YELLOW
c) GREEN
d) BLUE
e) WHITE

THE ANSWER IS b:

THE PART OF THE BUBBLE THAT
LOOKS BLUE IS DEFICIENT IN ITS
COMPLEMENTARY COLOR,
YELLOW.

Addison-Wesley Publishing Company, Inc.

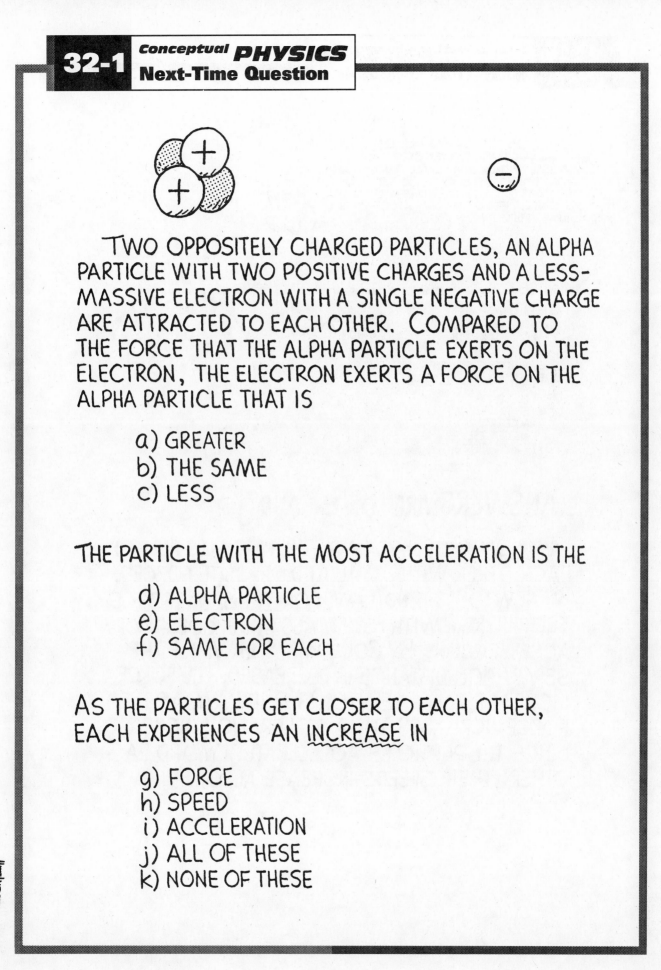

TWO OPPOSITELY CHARGED PARTICLES, AN ALPHA PARTICLE WITH TWO POSITIVE CHARGES AND A LESS-MASSIVE ELECTRON WITH A SINGLE NEGATIVE CHARGE ARE ATTRACTED TO EACH OTHER. COMPARED TO THE FORCE THAT THE ALPHA PARTICLE EXERTS ON THE ELECTRON, THE ELECTRON EXERTS A FORCE ON THE ALPHA PARTICLE THAT IS

a) GREATER
b) THE SAME
c) LESS

THE PARTICLE WITH THE MOST ACCELERATION IS THE

d) ALPHA PARTICLE
e) ELECTRON
f) SAME FOR EACH

AS THE PARTICLES GET CLOSER TO EACH OTHER, EACH EXPERIENCES AN <u>INCREASE</u> IN

g) FORCE
h) SPEED
i) ACCELERATION
j) ALL OF THESE
k) NONE OF THESE

TWO OPPOSITELY CHARGED PARTICLES, AN ALPHA PARTICLE WITH TWO POSITIVE CHARGES AND A LESS-MASSIVE ELECTRON WITH A SINGLE NEGATIVE CHARGE ARE ATTRACTED TO EACH OTHER. COMPARED TO THE FORCE THAT THE ALPHA PARTICLE EXERTS ON THE ELECTRON, THE ELECTRON EXERTS A FORCE ON THE ALPHA PARTICLE THAT IS

a) GREATER
b) THE SAME
c) LESS

THE PARTICLE WITH THE MOST ACCELERATION IS THE

d) ALPHA PARTICLE
e) ELECTRON
f) SAME FOR EACH

AS THE PARTICLES GET CLOSER TO EACH OTHER, EACH EXPERIENCES AN <u>INCREASE</u> IN

g) FORCE
h) SPEED
i) ACCELERATION
j) ALL OF THESE
k) NONE OF THESE

THE ANSWERS ARE b, e, AND j:

BY NEWTON'S 3RD LAW, THE PARTICLES PULL ON EACH OTHER WITH EQUAL AND OPPOSITE FORCES. BY NEWTON'S 2ND LAW, FOR THE SAME FORCE THE PARTICLE WITH LESS MASS UNDERGOES MORE ACCELERATION. BY COULOMB'S LAW, AS THE SEPARATION DISTANCE IS DECREASED, THE FORCE INCREASES. BY NEWTON'S 2ND LAW, AS THE FORCE INCREASES THE ACCELERATION INCREASES. SINCE THE PARTICLES ACCELERATE TOWARD EACH OTHER, THEIR SPEEDS INCREASE ALSO.

Addison-Wesley Publishing Company, Inc.

ARE OCCUPANTS OF AN AIRPLANE FLYING IN THE MIDST OF A THUNDER-STORM IN DANGER OF BEING STRUCK BY LIGHTNING?

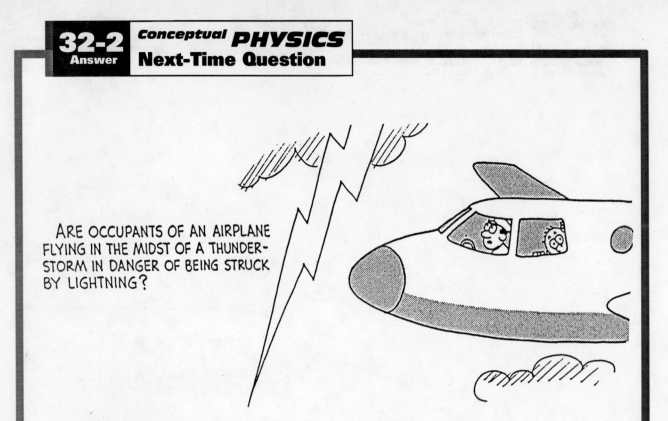

ARE OCCUPANTS OF AN AIRPLANE FLYING IN THE MIDST OF A THUNDER-STORM IN DANGER OF BEING STRUCK BY LIGHTNING?

ANSWER:

NO. SINCE THE PLANE DOES NOT OFFER A CONDUCTING PATH TO GROUND, IT IS UNLIKELY THAT IT WOULD BE STRUCK BY LIGHTNING. IF IT IS STRUCK, ELECTRIC CHARGES WILL MUTUALLY REPEL ONE ANOTHER AND NOT PENETRATE THE METAL SURFACE, WHICH ACTS AS AN ELECTRICAL SHIELD.

© 1997

A thin stream of water bends toward a negatively charged rod. When a positively charged rod is placed near the stream, it will bend in the

a) opposite direction.
b) same direction.
c) ...but it won't bend at all.

A thin stream of water bends toward a negatively charged rod. When a positively charged rod is placed near the stream, it will bend in the

a) opposite direction.
b) same direction.
c) ...but it won't bend at all.

Answer:

The answer is b. If you answered a, you likely thought the bending was due to positively charged water. But the water, even with many ions, normally has no appreciable net charge. The interaction between the charged rod and the water stream is mainly due to the dipole nature of water molecules. H_2O molecules are electric dipoles,

 positive on the hydrogen side and negative on the oxygen side. Like compasses that align along a magnetic field, H_2Os align along the electric field of the nearby rod -- whether the rod is positive or negative. For both magnets and charges, the closest aligned pole or charge is always opposite in sign. Opposites attract, so net attraction is the result.

Will a thin stream of kerosene bend in the presence of a charged rod?

Addison-Wesley Publishing Company, Inc.

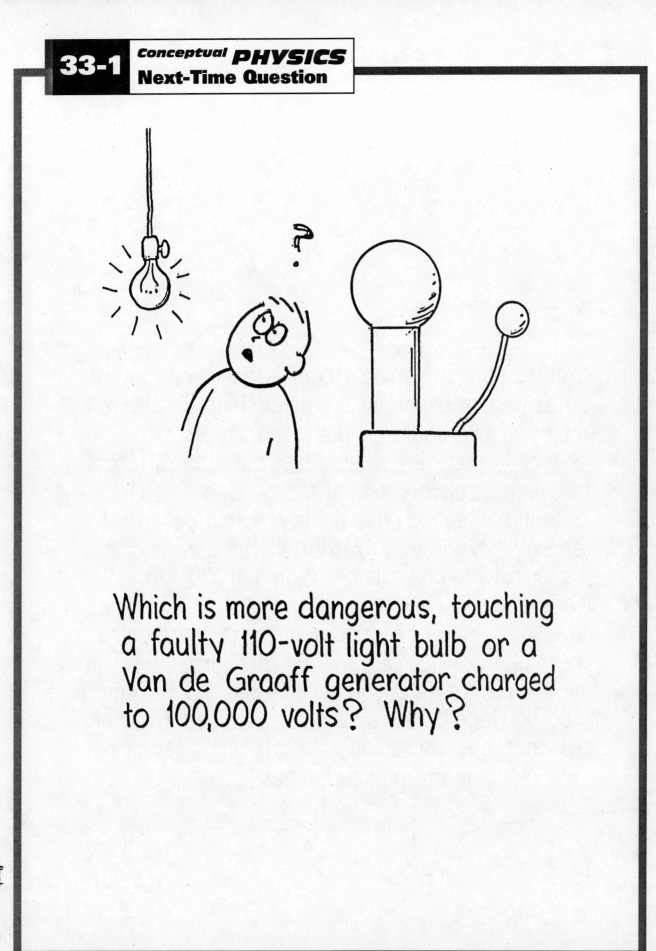

Which is more dangerous, touching a faulty 110-volt light bulb or a Van de Graaff generator charged to 100,000 volts? Why?

©1997

Which is more dangerous, touching a faulty 110-volt light bulb or a Van de Graaff generator charged to 100,000 volts? Why?

Answer:

Touching the Van de Graaff generator may be a hair-raising experience, but touching the 110-volt faulty fixture could be the last thing you do. The charged generator nicely illustrates the difference between electric potential energy and electric potential. Electric potential is electric potential energy *per charge*. Although the generator may be charged to an electric potential of 100,000 volts, the amount of charge is relatively small. That and the short time of charge transfer is why you're normally not harmed when it discharges through you. In contrast, if you become the shortcircuit for household 110 volts, the sustained transfer of charge is appreciable. Less energy per charge, but many, many more charges!

$$\frac{E}{q} = 110 \text{ V}$$

$$\frac{E}{q} = 100{,}000 \text{ V}$$

Addison-Wesley Publishing Company, Inc.

©1997

Electronics types don't take the force of gravity into account when calculating the trajectories of electrons in CRT tubes and the like. Why not?

Electronics types don't take the force of gravity into account when calculating the trajectories of electrons in CRT tubes and the like. Why not?

Answer:

Electronics engineers don't take the force of gravity into account only because of the small times involved with the customary short distances of electron trajectories. The electrons fall the same distances that baseballs would fall in the same time interval. The small mass of electrons doesn't alter the gravitational acceleration they experience—g. Even in the 2-mile long electron tube at the Stanford Linear Accelerator, for example, electrons complete their trip in less than 10^{-5} seconds, which at 9.8 m/s^2 finds them only 5×10^{-10} m (a few atomic diameters) below the straight-line path they would take without gravity. Gravitational acceleration g is still there—it's just that the time it acts is so small.

Addison-Wesley Publishing Company, Inc.

THE LAMP WILL NOT GLOW
WHEN IT IS HELD WITH BOTH ENDS
EQUIDISTANT FROM THE CHARGED
VAN DE GRAAFF GENERATOR. BUT
WHEN ONE END IS CLOSER TO THE
DOME THAN THE OTHER END, A
CURRENT IS ESTABLISHED AND IT
GLOWS. WHY?

THE LAMP WILL NOT GLOW
WHEN IT IS HELD WITH BOTH ENDS
EQUIDISTANT FROM THE CHARGED
VAN DE GRAAFF GENERATOR. BUT
WHEN ONE END IS CLOSER TO THE
DOME THAN THE OTHER END, A
CURRENT IS ESTABLISHED AND IT
GLOWS. WHY?

ANSWER:

SIMPLY PUT, THE END OF THE LAMP THAT IS HELD CLOSER TO THE DOME IS AT A HIGHER ELECTRIC POTENTIAL THAN THE FARTHER END. THE ELECTRIC POTENTIAL DIFFERENCE ACROSS THE ENDS OF THE LAMP PRODUCES A CURRENT IN THE LAMP.

MORE ACCURATELY, CHARGE ARCS FROM THE DOME THROUGH THE AIR TO THE CLOSEST PART OF THE LAMP, THEN THROUGH THE LAMP TO YOUR HAND, AND THEN THROUGH YOUR BODY TO THE FLOOR AND BACK TO THE GENERATOR TO FORM A CONTINUOUS LOOP. WHEN THE LAMP IS HELD IN THE FIRST POSITION, BOTH ENDS ARE EQUIDISTANT AND CHARGE DOES NOT FLOW THROUGH THE LENGTH OF THE LAMP TO COMPLETE THE CIRCUIT.

©1997

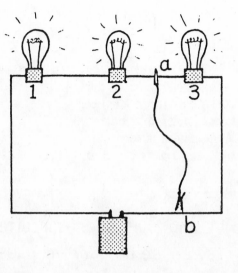

The simple series circuit consists of three identical lamps powered by battery. When a wire is connected between points *a* and *b*,

a) what happens to the brightness of lamp 3?

b) does current in the circuit increase, decrease, or remain the same?

c) what happens to the brightness of lamps 1 and 2?

d) does the voltage drop across lamps 1 and 2 increase, decrease, or remain the same?

e) is the power dissipated by the circuit increased, decreased, or does it remain the same?

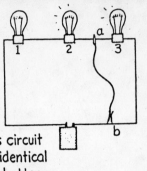

a) what happens to the brightness of lamp 3?

b) does current in the circuit increase, decrease, or remain the same?

c) what happens to the brightness of lamps 1 and 2?

d) does the voltage drop across lamps 1 and 2 increase, decrease, or remain the same?

e) is the power dissipated by the circuit increased, decreased, or does it remain the same?

The simple series circuit consists of three identical lamps powered by battery. When a wire is connected between points *a* and *b*,

Answers:

a) Lamp 3 is short-circuited. It no longer glows because no current passes through it.

b) The current in the circuit increases. Why? Because the circuit resistance is reduced. Whereas charge was made to flow through three lamps before, now it flows through only two lamps -- $\frac{2}{3}$ the resistance results in $\frac{3}{2}$ the current (neglecting temperature effects).

c) Lamps 1 and 2 glow brighter because of the increased current through them.

d) The voltage drop across lamps 1 and 2 is greater. Whereas voltage supplied by the battery was previously divided between three lamps, it is now divided between only two lamps. So more energy is now given to each lamp.

e) The power output of the two-lamp circuit is greater because of the greater current. This means more light will be emitted by the two lamps in series than from the three lamps in series. Three lamps connected in parallel, however, put out more light. Lamps are most often connected in parallel.

©1997 Paul G. Hewitt

THE 40-WATT BULB AND THE
100-WATT BULB ARE CONNECTED
IN SERIES TO THE BATTERY.
WHICH BULB WILL GLOW BRIGHTER?

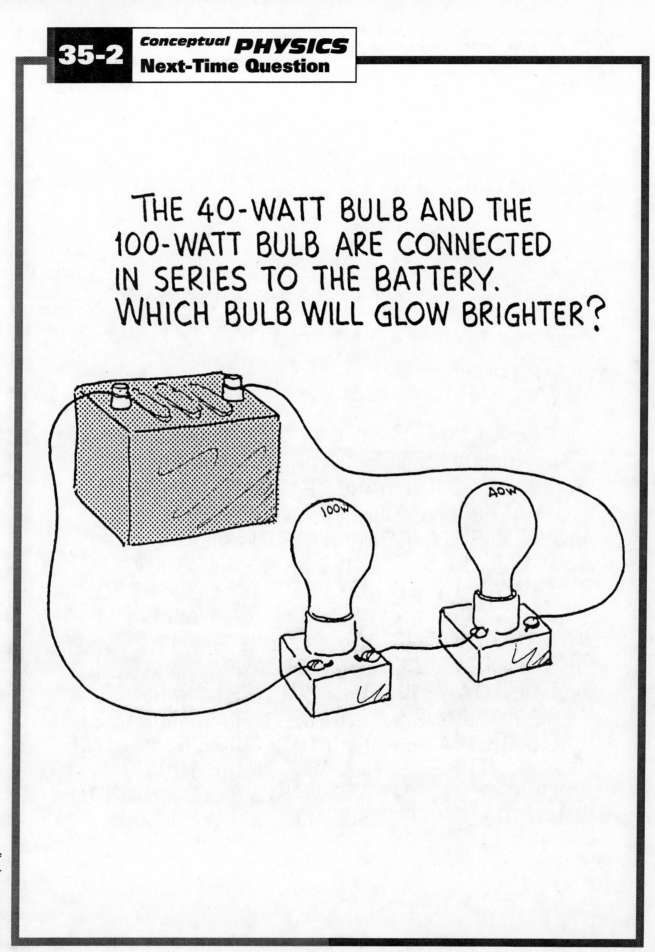

THE 40-WATT BULB AND THE
100-WATT BULB ARE CONNECTED
IN SERIES TO THE BATTERY.
WHICH BULB WILL GLOW BRIGHTER?

ANSWER:

THE 40-WATT BULB WILL GLOW BRIGHTER WHEN
CONNECTED IN SERIES. TO UNDERSTAND THIS YOU
MUST FIRST UNDERSTAND THAT THE FILAMENT IN A
40-WATT BULB IS THINNER AND THEREFORE OF
HIGHER RESISTANCE THAN THE FILAMENT OF A
100-WATT BULB. IT IS THE HIGHER RESISTANCE OF
THE 40-WATT BULB THAT KEEPS THE CURRENT TO
ONLY 40/100 THE CURRENT IN A 100-WATT BULB
WHEN BOTH ARE PROPERLY CONNECTED IN *PARALLEL*.
THEN MORE CURRENT FLOWS IN THE 100-WATT BULB
AND IT GLOWS BRIGHTER. BUT WHEN CONNECTED IN
SERIES, THE CURRENT IS LESS BUT IS THE SAME IN
EACH. THE SAME AMOUNT OF CURRENT "SQUEEZING"
THROUGH THE FINER FILAMENT OF THE 40-WATT
BULB HEATS IT MORE AND MAKES IT GLOW BRIGHTER
THAN THE LOWER-RESISTANCE 100-WATT BULB.

Addison-Wesley Publishing Company, Inc.

Which circuit draws the most current?

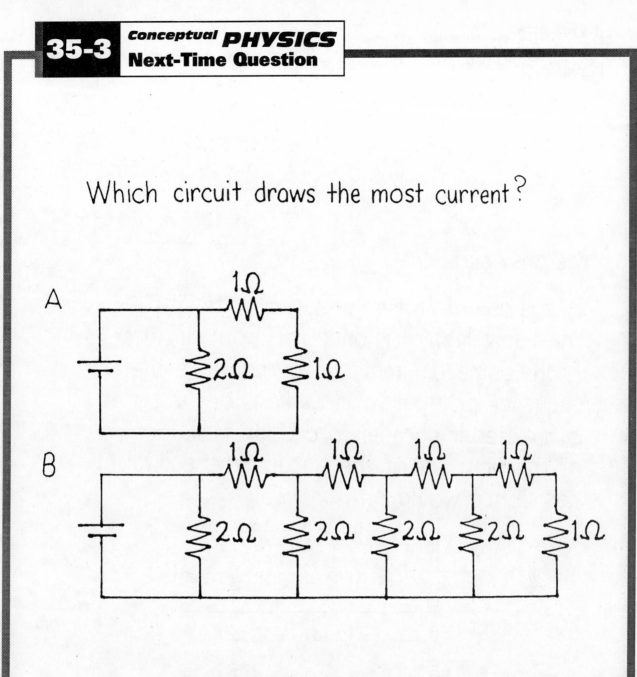

A

1Ω

2Ω   1Ω

B

1Ω   1Ω   1Ω   1Ω

2Ω 2Ω 2Ω 2Ω 1Ω

a) Circuit A

b) Circuit B

c) Both the same

Which circuit draws the most current?

a) Circuit A
b) Circuit B
c) Both the same

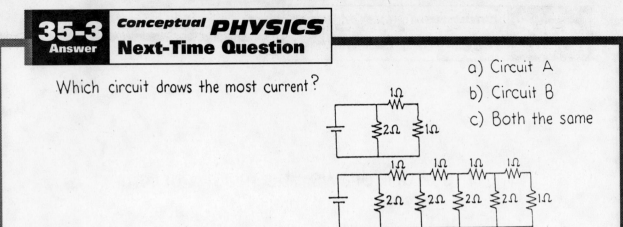

The answer is c:

This is one of those "tricky" circuits wherein the equivalent resistance for both circuits is the same. In fact, if you continue the sequence of a pair of 1-Ω resistors in series connected in parallel to a 2-Ω resistor at the right end of the circuit, the equivalent resistance would still be 1 Ω.

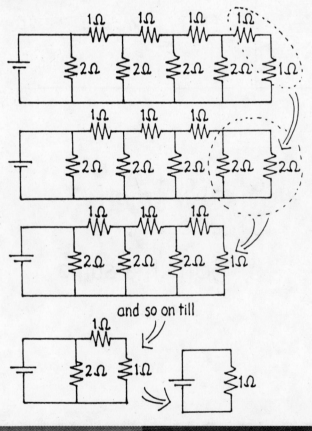

and so on till

Addison-Wesley Publishing Company, Inc.

Compared to the huge force that attracts an iron tack to a strong magnet, the force that the tack exerts on the magnet is

a) relatively small

b) equally huge

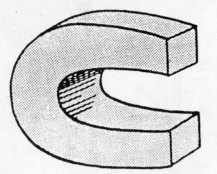

Compared to the huge force that attracts an iron tack to a strong magnet, the force that the tack exerts on the magnet is

a) relatively small

b) equally huge

Answer:

The pair of forces between the tack and magnet comprises a single interaction and both are equal in magnitude and opposite in direction-Newton's third law.

Like which pulls harder on the stretched rubber band – my thumb or my finger?

©1997

Addison-Wesley Publishing Company, Inc.

THE TWO IRON BARS LOOK ALIKE, BUT ONLY ONE IS A MAGNET. HOW CAN YOU DETERMINE WHICH IS THE MAGNET ONLY BY INVESTIGATING THEIR INTERACTION WITH EACH OTHER?

THE TWO IRON BARS LOOK ALIKE, BUT ONLY ONE IS A MAGNET. HOW CAN YOU DETERMINE WHICH IS THE MAGNET ONLY BY INVESTIGATING THEIR INTERACTION WITH EACH OTHER?

SOLUTION:

MAKE A **T** SHAPE WITH THE BARS. ONLY WHEN THE MAGNET IS PLACED AT THE MID-POINT OF THE NON-MAGNET WILL THEY STICK!

©1997

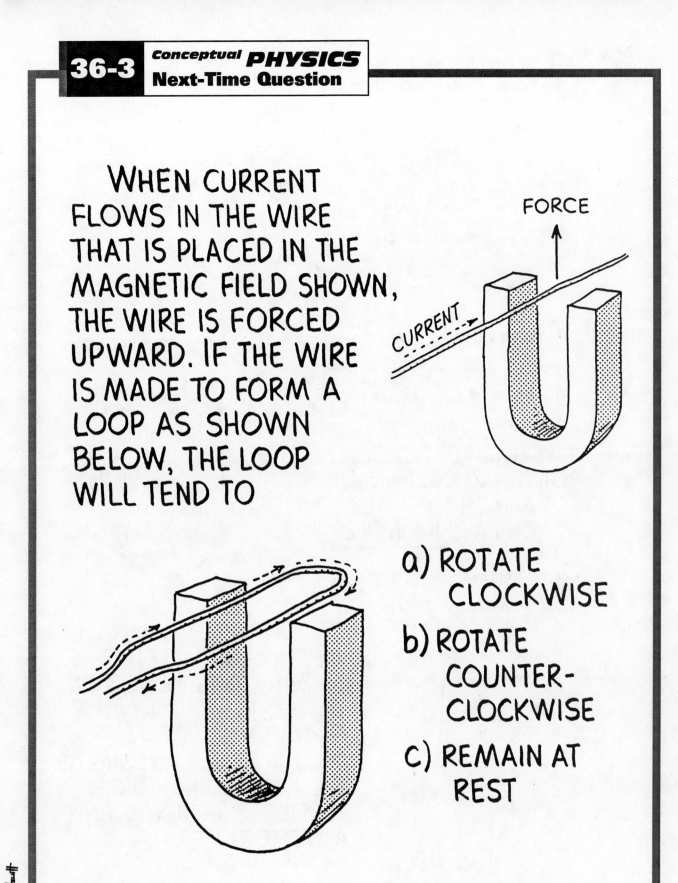

WHEN CURRENT FLOWS IN THE WIRE THAT IS PLACED IN THE MAGNETIC FIELD SHOWN, THE WIRE IS FORCED UPWARD. IF THE WIRE IS MADE TO FORM A LOOP AS SHOWN BELOW, THE LOOP WILL TEND TO

FORCE

CURRENT

a) ROTATE CLOCKWISE

b) ROTATE COUNTER-CLOCKWISE

c) REMAIN AT REST

©1997

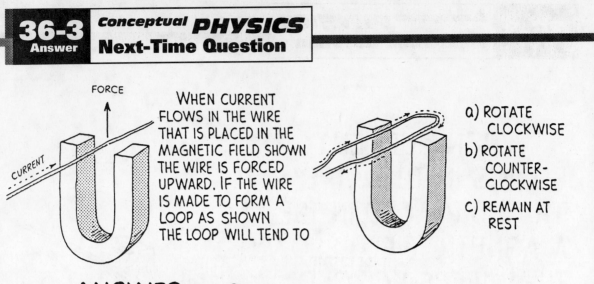

FORCE

CURRENT

WHEN CURRENT FLOWS IN THE WIRE THAT IS PLACED IN THE MAGNETIC FIELD SHOWN THE WIRE IS FORCED UPWARD. IF THE WIRE IS MADE TO FORM A LOOP AS SHOWN THE LOOP WILL TEND TO

a) ROTATE CLOCKWISE

b) ROTATE COUNTER-CLOCKWISE

c) REMAIN AT REST

THE ANSWER IS a:

THE LEFT SIDE IS FORCED UP WHILE THE RIGHT SIDE IS FORCED DOWN AS SHOWN. IF YOU MAKE THE LOOP ROTATE AGAINST A SPRING AND ATTACH A POINTER TO IT, YOU HAVE A SIMPLE ELECTRIC METER. AT MAXIMUM, IT CAN ONLY MAKE A HALF TURN.

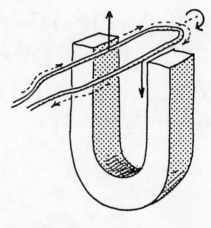

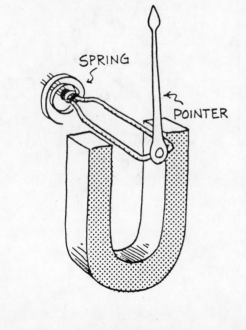

SPRING

POINTER

BUT IF YOU MAKE THE CURRENT CHANGE DIRECTION (ALTERNATE) AT EVERY HALF TURN, IT WILL ROTATE CONTINUOUSLY AS LONG AS THE ALTERNATING CURRENT PERSISTS. THEN YOU HAVE A MOTOR.

©1997

WHAT HAPPENS TO THE READING ON THE GALVANOMETER WHEN THE SWITCH IN CIRCUIT 1 IS a) FIRST CLOSED, b) KEPT CLOSED, AND c) OPENED AGAIN?

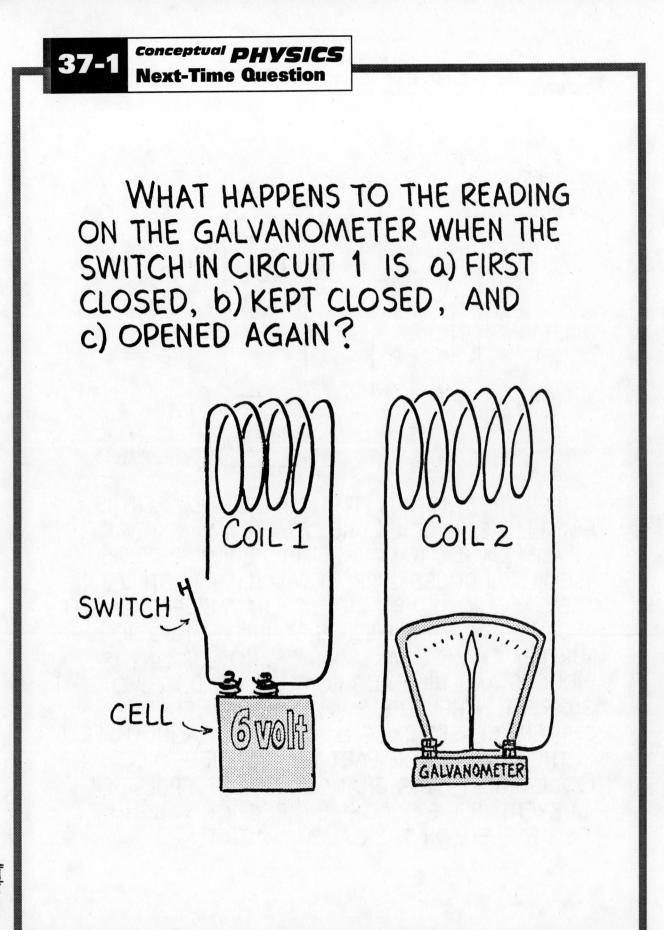

©1997

WHAT HAPPENS TO THE READING ON THE GALVANOMETER WHEN THE SWITCH IN CIRCUIT 1 IS a) FIRST CLOSED, b) KEPT CLOSED, AND c) OPENED AGAIN?

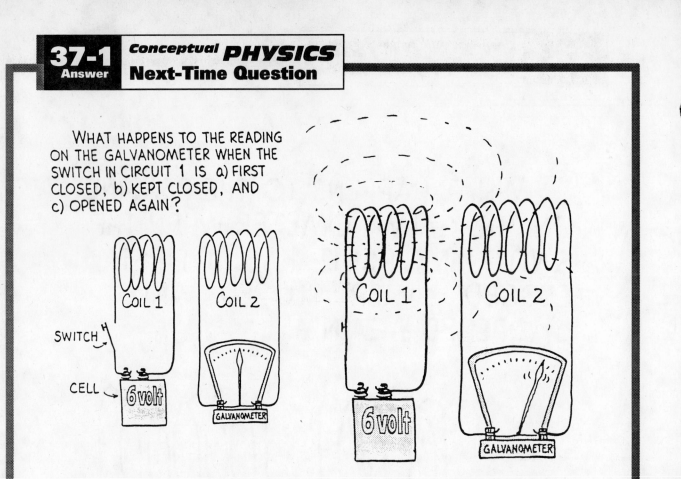

WHEN THE SWITCH IS FIRST CLOSED, A CURRENT IS ESTABLISHED IN COIL 1 AND CREATES A MAGNETIC FIELD WHICH EXTENDS TO COIL 2. THIS BUILD-UP OF FIELD IN COIL 2 INDUCES CURRENT WHICH IS REGISTERED IN THE GALVANOMETER. THE CURRENT IS BRIEF, HOWEVER, BECAUSE ONCE THE FIELD IS STABILIZED AND NO FURTHER CHANGE TAKES PLACE, NO CURRENT IS INDUCED AND THE GALVANOMETER READS ZERO CURRENT. WHEN THE SWITCH IS OPENED, THE CURRENT CEASES IN COIL 1 AND THE MAGNETIC FIELD IN THE COIL AND THE PART THAT EXTENDS TO COIL 2 COLLAPSES. THIS CHANGE INDUCES A PULSE OF CURRENT IN THE OPPOSITE DIRECTION WHICH IS REGISTERED ON THE GALVANOMETER.

Addison-Wesley Publishing Company, Inc.

WHEN THE ZINC BALL ON THE
CHARGED ELECTROSCOPE IS
ILLUMINATED WITH ULTRAVIOLET
LIGHT, THE LEAVES OF THE
ELECTROSCOPE COLLAPSE.
WAS THE ELECTROSCOPE
CHARGED POSITIVE, OR NEGATIVE?

WHEN THE ZINC BALL ON THE
CHARGED ELECTROSCOPE IS
ILLUMINATED WITH ULTRAVIOLET
LIGHT, THE LEAVES OF THE
ELECTROSCOPE COLLAPSE.
WAS THE ELECTROSCOPE
CHARGED POSITIVE, OR NEGATIVE?

ANSWER:

THE ELECTROSCOPE WAS DISCHARGED BY
THE PHOTOELECTRIC EFFECT. UV LIGHT
INCIDENT UPON THE ZINC DISLODGED
ELECTRONS INTO THE AIR. HENCE THE
ELECTROSCOPE MUST HAVE BEEN NEGATIVELY
CHARGED. IF IT WERE POSITIVELY CHARGED,
THE DISLODGING OF ELECTRONS WOULD
HAVE MADE IT MORE POSITIVELY CHARGED,
NOT LESS CHARGED. INCIDENTALLY, IF
GLASS WERE PLACED BETWEEN THE UV
SOURCE AND THE ZINC, NO DISCHARGE
WOULD OCCUR. WHY? BECAUSE GLASS
ACTS AS A FILTER FOR UV LIGHT.

©1997

Addison-Wesley Publishing Company, Inc.

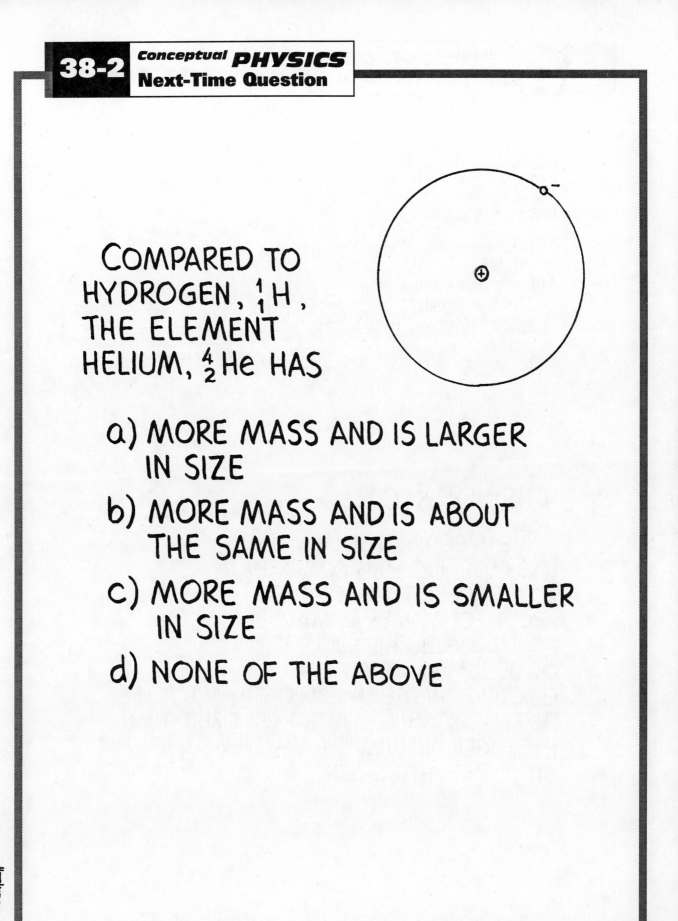

COMPARED TO HYDROGEN, $^1_1$H, THE ELEMENT HELIUM, $^4_2$He HAS

a) MORE MASS AND IS LARGER IN SIZE

b) MORE MASS AND IS ABOUT THE SAME IN SIZE

c) MORE MASS AND IS SMALLER IN SIZE

d) NONE OF THE ABOVE

©1997

COMPARED TO
HYDROGEN, $^1_1$H,
THE ELEMENT
HELIUM, $^4_2$He HAS

a) MORE MASS AND IS LARGER
   IN SIZE
b) MORE MASS AND IS ABOUT
   THE SAME IN SIZE
c) MORE MASS AND IS SMALLER
   IN SIZE
d) NONE OF THE ABOVE

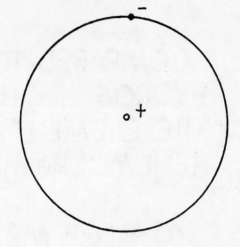

THE ANSWER IS C:

THE NUCLEUS OF HELIUM
HAS FOUR NUCLEONS COMPARED
TO HYDROGEN'S ONE, SO IT IS
ABOUT FOUR TIMES AS MASSIVE
AS HYDROGEN. THE NUCLEUS
OF HELIUM HAS TWICE THE
ELECTRIC CHARGE OF HYDROGEN, AND PULLS
ITS ELECTRONS INTO A TIGHTER ORBIT THAN
HYDROGEN. HELIUM IS A SMALLER BUT HEAVIER
ATOM THAN HYDROGEN.

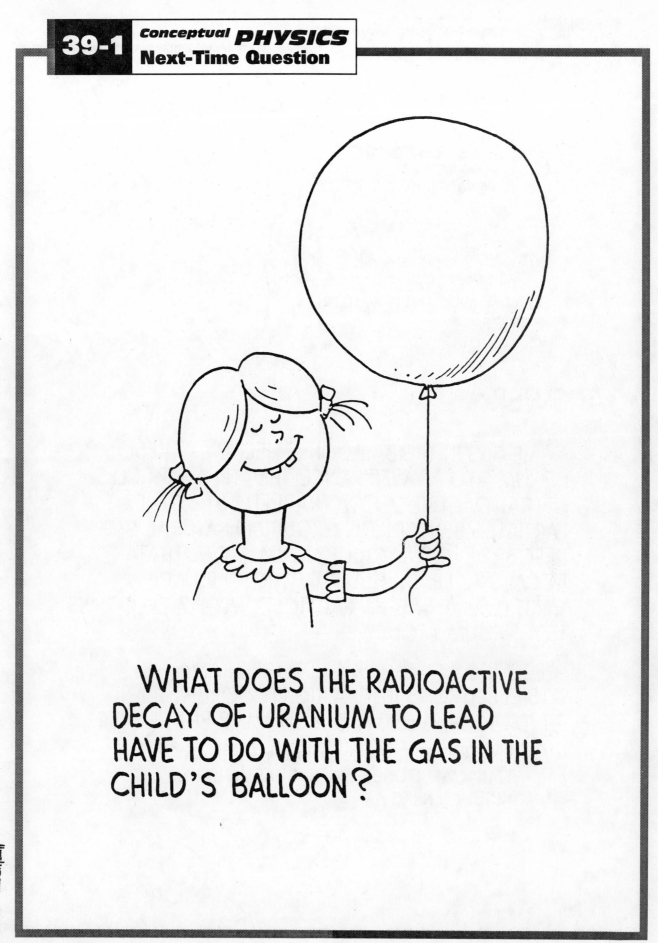

WHAT DOES THE RADIOACTIVE
DECAY OF URANIUM TO LEAD
HAVE TO DO WITH THE GAS IN THE
CHILD'S BALLOON?

©1997

WHAT DOES THE RADIOACTIVE
DECAY OF URANIUM TO LEAD
HAVE TO DO WITH THE GAS IN THE
CHILD'S BALLOON?

ANSWER:

THE GAS IN THE BALLOON IS HELIUM. THESE
HELIUM ATOMS WERE ONCE THE ALPHA PARTICLES
OF RADIOACTIVE DECAY TRAPPED WITH OTHER
PARTICLES BENEATH THE GROUND IN NATURAL GAS
DEPOSITS. FOR EACH URANIUM ATOM THAT
DECAYS TO LEAD, 8 ALPHA PARTICLES ARE
EMITTED. AN ALPHA PARTICLE WITH 2 ELECTRONS
IS A HELIUM ATOM.

LIKE A CANNONBALL, AN ALPHA PARTICLE
IS HARMFUL ONLY WHEN IT HAS A HIGH
KINETIC ENERGY.

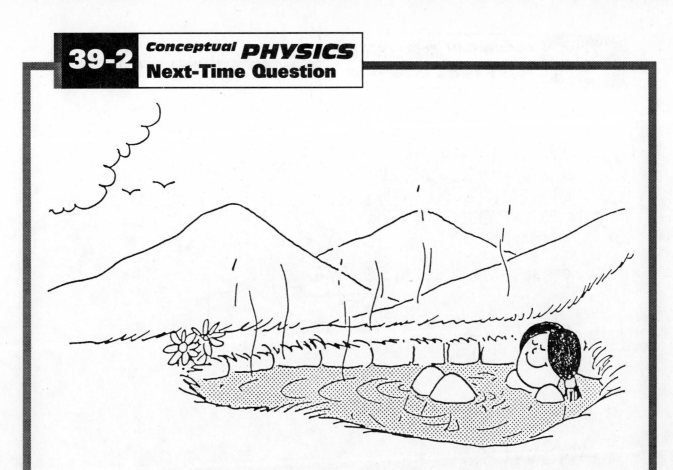

SHE BATHES IN THE WARMTH OF A
NATURAL HOT SPRING LOCATED IN THE
QUIET AND PEACEFUL MOUNTAINS.
INTERESTINGLY ENOUGH, THE SPRING
WATER IS WARMED BY

a) FIRES BENEATH THE EARTH'S SURFACE
b) THE EARTH'S OWN NATURAL HEAT
c) SOLAR POWER
d) NUCLEAR POWER

©1997

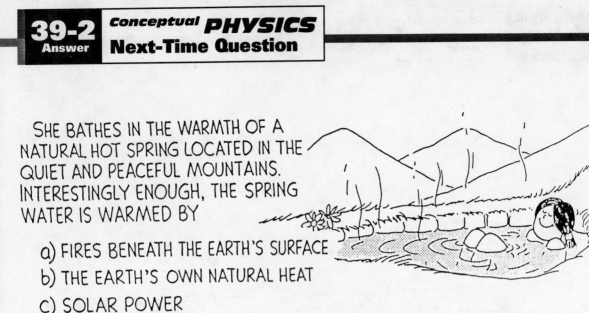

SHE BATHES IN THE WARMTH OF A
NATURAL HOT SPRING LOCATED IN THE
QUIET AND PEACEFUL MOUNTAINS.
INTERESTINGLY ENOUGH, THE SPRING
WATER IS WARMED BY

a) FIRES BENEATH THE EARTH'S SURFACE
b) THE EARTH'S OWN NATURAL HEAT
c) SOLAR POWER
d) NUCLEAR POWER

ANSWER:

THE SPRING IS WARMED BY NUCLEAR POWER --
NOT FROM NUCLEAR POWER PLANTS THAT
GENERATE ELECTRICITY -- BUT FROM THE NATURAL
RADIOACTIVE DECAY OF ATOMIC NUCLEI IN
THE EARTH'S INTERIOR. RADIOACTIVITY IS THE
SOURCE OF THE EARTH'S "OWN NATURAL HEAT,"
WHICH PRODUCES HOT SPRINGS -- AND
GEYSERS AS WELL.

THIS DOESN'T MEAN THAT HOT SPRINGS
AND GEYSERS THEMSELVES ARE RADIOACTIVE.
THEIR THERMAL ENERGY IS SIMPLY A BYPRODUCT
OF NUCLEAR DECAY DEEP BENEATH THE EARTH'S
SURFACE.

©1997

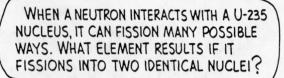

WHEN A NEUTRON INTERACTS WITH A U-235 NUCLEUS, IT CAN FISSION MANY POSSIBLE WAYS. WHAT ELEMENT RESULTS IF IT FISSIONS INTO TWO IDENTICAL NUCLEI?

CAN YOU ANSWER THIS ONE? HOW MANY NEUTRONS ARE PRODUCED WHEN A U-235 NUCLEUS FISSIONS INTO Sr-90 AND Xe-138?

ANSWERS:

IF URANIUM FISSIONS INTO TWO IDENTICAL ELEMENTS, THEIR ATOMIC NUMBER IS HALF 92, OR 46. THAT'S PALLADIUM.

IF U-235 FISSIONS INTO STRONTIUM-90 AND XENON-138, 8 NEUTRONS ARE RELEASED, ACCORDING TO THE REACTION

$$^{235}_{92}U + ^{1}_{0}n \longrightarrow ^{90}_{38}Sr + ^{138}_{54}Xe + 8(^{1}_{0}n).$$

(THE NUMBER OF NEUTRONS RELEASED PER FISSION REACTION FOR MOST REACTIONS IS CONSIDERABLY LESS THAN 8.)

©1997

$$^2_1\text{H} + {}^2_1\text{H} \rightarrow {}^3_2\text{He} + (\quad\quad)$$

$$^2_1\text{H} + {}^3_1\text{H} \rightarrow {}^4_2\text{He} + (\quad\quad)$$

$$^3_1\text{H} + (\quad\quad) \rightarrow {}^4_2\text{He} + {}^1_0\text{n} + {}^1_0\text{n}$$

©1997

SOME COMMON FUSION
REACTIONS OF HYDROGEN
ISOTOPES ARE SHOWN
IN INCOMPLETE FORM
BELOW. CAN YOU
COMPLETE THEM?

$$^2_1H + {}^2_1H \rightarrow {}^3_2He + (\quad)$$

$$^2_1H + {}^3_1H \rightarrow {}^4_2He + (\quad)$$

$$^3_1H + (\quad) \rightarrow {}^4_2He + {}^1_0n + {}^1_0n$$

ANSWERS:

$$^2_1H + {}^2_1H \longrightarrow {}^3_2He + {}^1_0n$$

$$^2_1H + {}^3_1H \longrightarrow {}^4_2He + {}^1_0n$$

$$^3_1H + {}^3_1H \longrightarrow {}^4_2He + {}^1_0n + {}^1_0n$$

Addison-Wesley Publishing Company, Inc.

SAILING IS FUN, ESPECIALLY ON A WINDY DAY. CONSIDER THE TOP VIEWS OF THE TWO BOATS BELOW, ONE SAILING WITH THE WIND, AND THE OTHER ACROSS THE WIND. WHICH CAN SAIL FASTER THAN WIND SPEED?

WIND

SAILING IS FUN, ESPECIALLY ON A WINDY DAY. CONSIDER THE TOP VIEWS OF THE TWO BOATS BELOW, ONE SAILING WITH THE WIND, AND THE OTHER ACROSS THE WIND. WHICH CAN SAIL FASTER THAN WIND SPEED?

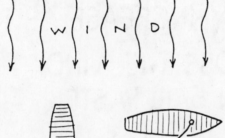

ANSWER:

THE BOAT THAT SAILS DIRECTLY WITH THE WIND CAN SAIL NO FASTER THAN WIND SPEED. WHY? EVEN SAILING AS FAST AS THE WIND, THERE WOULD BE NO WIND IMPACT AGAINST THE SAIL. IT WOULD SAG. BUT WHEN SAILING CROSSWIND, THERE WOULD STILL BE WIND IMPACT AGAINST THE SAIL, AND SPEEDS GREATER THAN WIND SPEED CAN BE ACHIEVED.

(WHY WILL THE SAIL ALSO SAG WHEN AT AN ANGLE OF 45° AND THE BOAT TRAVELS CROSS-WIND AT WIND SPEED?)

©1997

Addison-Wesley Publishing Company, Inc.

WE ALL KNOW THAT THE FORCE OF
WIND IMPACT DRIVES A SAILBOAT.
IN WHICH OF THE THREE POSITIONS
DOES THE WIND IMPACT FORCE
ACTUALLY INCREASE AS THE BOAT
MOVES FASTER?

WE ALL KNOW THAT THE FORCE OF WIND IMPACT DRIVES A SAILBOAT. IN WHICH OF THE THREE POSITIONS DOES THE WIND IMPACT FORCE ACTUALLY INCREASE AS THE BOAT MOVES FASTER?

W I N D

a   b   c

ANSWER:

JUST AS RAINDROPS HIT YOU HARDER THE FASTER YOU RUN INTO A SLANTING RAIN, THE WIND IMPACT INCREASES FOR BOAT **C** THAT ANGLES INTO THE WIND. FOR THIS REASON, A SAILCRAFT ATTAINS MAXIMUM SPEED WHEN DIRECTED AT AN ANGLE UPWIND RATHER THAN CROSSWIND OR DOWNWIND. IT CAN'T SAIL DIRECTLY UPWIND, BUT IT CAN SAIL TO A DESTINATION UPWIND BY ZIG-ZAGGING BACK AND FORTH. THIS IS CALLED *TACKING*.

   Addison-Wesley Publishing Company, Inc.

SUPPOSE THE HEIGHT OF A RAPIDLY-GROWING BEANSTALK DOUBLES EACH DAY, AND IN 36 DAYS REACHES THE MOON. HOW MANY DAYS DOES IT TAKE TO GET HALF WAY TO THE MOON?

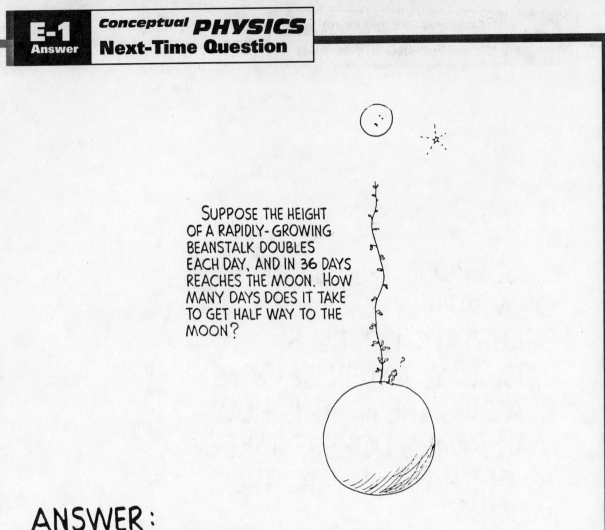

SUPPOSE THE HEIGHT OF A RAPIDLY-GROWING BEANSTALK DOUBLES EACH DAY, AND IN 36 DAYS REACHES THE MOON. HOW MANY DAYS DOES IT TAKE TO GET HALF WAY TO THE MOON?

ANSWER:

35 DAYS! IF IT TOOK 36 DAYS FOR THE BEAN-STALK TO REACH THE MOON, AND IT DOUBLES IN HEIGHT EACH DAY, THEN IT REACHED HALF WAY TO THE MOON ON THE 35TH DAY (AND ONE-QUARTER THE DISTANCE TO THE MOON ON THE 34TH DAY). THIS WORKS BACKWARD TO A STALK SLIGHTLY MORE THAN 1cm HIGH ON THE FIRST DAY!

Addison-Wesley Publishing Company, Inc.